P³H:
Pilots, Passengers, Prisoners & Hijackers

Trish Hatch, PhD

P³H: Pilots, Passengers, Prisoners & Hijackers

Copyright © 2018 Trish Hatch, PhD

All rights reserved. No part of this book may be reproduced in any manner without written permission from the author.

ISBN – 1-7324269-0-0

www.hatchingresults.com

Printed in the United States of America

CONTENTS

Preface / vii
Pre-flight Information / viii

SECTION I
INTRODUCING THE ARCHETYPES

CHAPTER 1   The P^{3}H Flight Test / 2

CHAPTER 2   Archetype Profiles / 9
                   I am a pilot
                   I am a passenger
                   I am a prisoner
                   I am a hijacker

SECTION II
WORKING WITH YOUR FELLOW FLYERS

CHAPTER 3   Flying With Pilots / 22
                   What Pilots Have to Offer
                   Strategies for Working With Pilots

CHAPTER 4   Flying With Passengers / 27
                   What Passengers Have to Offer
                   Strategies for Working With Passengers

CHAPTER 5   Flying With Prisoners / 33
                   What Prisoners Have to Offer
                   Strategies for Working With Prisoners

CHAPTER 6   Flying With Hijackers / 39
                   What Hijackers Have to Offer
                   Strategies for Working With Hijackers
                   Special Case: Hijackers Who Think
                       They Are Pilots

CONTENTS, cont.

SECTION III
MANAGING THE FLIGHT

CHAPTER 7 **Other Fellow Passengers / 55**
- Copilots
- "Wannabe" Pilots
- Newborns
- Flight Attendants
- Passengers in the Emergency Row
- Transportation Security Administration (TSA) Officers

CHAPTER 8 **Lessons, Questions, and Comments from the Field / 61**
- No Copilot for Me!
- Reluctant Pilots
- Potential Hijackers
- Pilot "Secretaries"
- Parachuting
- Changing Roles

CHAPTER 9 **So You Want to Be A Pilot? / 67**
- Excellence in Leadership
- Grooming New Pilots
- Pushing Passengers Too Hard
- If You Are on the Wrong Plane, *Get Off*
- Get Commitment from the Squadron Before Taking Off
- Managing the Mission

CHAPTER 10 **The Right Formula / 71**
- What is the "Right" Formula?
- Too Many Pilots?
- Not Enough Pilots?
- Too Many Prisoners?
- Too Many Hijackers?

CONTENTS, cont.

APPENDICES

APPENDIX I Activity Worksheets / 76
Activity 1: Who upsets you the most?
Activity 2: Who do you know who is ... ?
Activity 3: What has worked?
Activity 4: What has not worked?
Activity 5: This week I'll try...
Activity 6: Where is your plane headed?
Activity 7: Different Situations
Activity 8: My Pilot Improvement Worksheet

APPENDIX II What Do Flyers FEEL?
What Do Flyers WANT? / 84

ACKNOWLEDGMENTS/RESOURCES / 94

PREFACE

BOARDING PASS

Years ago, I agreed to leave a rewarding central office administrative position to become an administrator at a large, diverse, underperforming school. I was charged with creating systemic change. It was a fabulously enlightening year. What I learned in that one year about how to work with difficult people will continue to guide my work in education for the rest of my career and has contributed greatly to this book. While some of the characters in this book are loosely based on staff members at this site, others are combinations of either central office personnel I worked with and for, or people I encountered during my work in state and national professional organizations. They are archetypes that could certainly be found in any business or organization attempting to "move forward."

FLIGHT: P3H-001
DEPARTURE TIME: NOW
DESTINATION: SUCCESS

BOARDING PASS

PRE-FLIGHT INFORMATION

As a national trainer in reforming school counseling programs, I am often asked if I have advice for educators looking to serve as change agents in schools. They seek assistance on how to work more effectively with staff who resist change or thwart their efforts to use data to effect change; become systems and student advocates; and be more effective leaders in schools, districts, and professional organizations.

Recently, the school counseling profession has undergone great change; it is moving toward a focus on academic achievement and career and college access for every K–12 student. Just as others have worked to improve education by aligning standards to curriculum and collecting results of their programs and services, school counselors and their programs have attempted to "move forward." This book is a guide to help educators and other leaders support all staff members in dealing with change in schools and organizations; in particular, it addresses the resistance and sabotage that inevitably arise in response to change, among at least a few staff members.

By learning more about the motivations that guide the behaviors of staff within the educational system, leaders can access their ability to safely fly their plane in the direction of successful and equitable change. By utilizing the P^3H (pilots, passengers, prisoners, and hijackers) metaphor, a leader in a school building or district, educational system, professional association, or other organizational system that strives to move forward will be able to classify school and district staff and/or organization members according to their agendas, needs, and abilities. Some of these individuals (pilots) possess a tremendous interest in helping to move the system forward; some (passengers) are along for the ride. Still others (prisoners) are on the plane because they have no choice (they feel trapped)—and finally some (hijackers) are on board to sabotage change, to protect their interests and ensure that they block forward motion at all costs.

Throughout this book, the airplane metaphor is applied as a powerful tool for change. I completed it while sitting on an airplane en route from

Manchester, New Hampshire, to Washington Dulles International Airport, and now I respectfully offer this guide to educators seeking greater success in equitable change, advocacy, and leadership in school systems and professional organizations. I use the airplane metaphor to honor the inspiration found in the heroism of those passengers who, in the face of hijackers, became pilots (and heroes) on 9/11, and their affect on inspiring systemic change in the United States. It's that kind of courage we need today in education if we are going to make the changes necessary for equity in K–12 schools.

P³H is an approach to leading and managing difficult (and sometimes dangerous) people. If you are one of the many educators navigating through unfriendly skies and trying to change the world in these difficult educational times, then this book is written for you. It begins in Section I, with a quiz that introduces you to each archetype through many examples, and Chapter 2 describes each archetype in detail. In Section II, Chapters 3–6 discuss working with each archetype, including several strategies for managing and making the most of what each has to offer. Section III covers approaches to managing your flight. Chapter 7 covers other people on the plane, Chapter 8 includes some questions and answers from educators who have attended my workshops, and Chapter 9 describes how truly effective leaders fly their planes. Chapter 10 discusses research into the correlation between use of the P³H model and student achievement in schools, as well as strategies for balancing the numbers of each archetype in a school.

Two appendices provide activities for educators wanting to move forward using this aeronautical metaphor. Appendix I includes eight worksheets to help staff and leadership assess their feelings and activities from this perspective. Appendix II summarizes the feelings and desires of the four archetypes and provides suggestions for discussion.

Learning how to recognize the P³H archetypes is the first step; knowing how to manage them is the key to success as a leader.

—Trish Hatch, PhD

"It doesn't cost money to change attitudes."
–Stephanie Robinson, Education Trust Principal Partner Emerita

1
Introducing the Archetypes

In this section you will learn what each of the archetypes have to offer and strategies you can use to work with each one.

1 The P³H Flight Test

The 3 P's are Pilots, Passengers, and Prisoners; H is for Hijackers.

Imagine your boss (in this case, the principal) calls an emergency staff meeting. Your response to this request might be that you arrive early to get a good seat, because you don't want to miss any important information. Or perhaps you come with no particular enthusiasm and decide to sit with friends wherever they are and act polite, because it's part of the job. Maybe you hate going, but since they are taking attendance, you know you have to but grumble in the back that these meetings are boring and a waste of time. Finally, perhaps you decide not to go and you coerce others not to as well.

Recognize any of these responses? They are often represented in schools. If you are a leader in education or attempting to create systemic change in an organizational system, it is vital to prepare to deal with these responses. You must know why, when and how to act with various members of your school, district staff, or organization, and be prepared to react to their behaviors in ways that will keep the change process moving forward.

Here is a simple quiz to get started on P³H archetypes. The following scenarios are taken from my experiences working in schools, and responses have been categorized to provide an introduction to and examples of each of the archetypes: (a) pilots, (b) passengers, (c) prisoners, and (d) hijackers. Notice your first thoughts and feelings about each archetype and example. Next, notice your thoughts and feelings about staff members in your current school, or organization who might respond in each of the ways described. Don't be surprised if you recall former staff and former schools, districts, and organizations, as well.

THE P³H FLIGHT TEST

1. **Your district announces there is training for school counselors on the ASCA National Model (or some other new program). Your response:**

    - ☐ a. "This sounds interesting. I'm always looking to improve my work."
    - ☐ b. "If everyone's going, I guess I'll go—who knows, it might be ok."
    - ☐ c. "I'm not attending this. It's a waste of time, and these trainings are always boring. I'll only go if they make me—and I better get paid for it. I'll see if the union says I have to go."
    - ☐ d. "Oh, so they think they're going to bring in something new, do they? Well, not while I'm still here. I'd better find out what this is.... We're not doing it unless I agree."

2. **New textbooks are being reviewed for adoption. Your response:**

    - ☐ a. You volunteer to help review them, because making a good choice is important.
    - ☐ b. You tell the department chair she ought to go because you trust her to do the right thing.
    - ☐ c. "They're changing my textbook again? Are they nuts? That's *it*; I'm putting in for early retirement!"
    - ☐ d. "They can change it if they want, but in *my* classroom, I'll teach what *I decide* to teach."

3. **A national conference is coming to a city near your district. Your response:**

    - ☐ a. "I'm registering right away—I can't wait to get new ideas for the department."
    - ☐ b. "If everyone is going, I guess I'll go."
    - ☐ c. "Conferences are a waste of time—I'll go if they make me, but I'll just go shopping instead of attending the sessions."
    - ☐ d. "I'll go to see what they're up to, because they don't run things around here." [*Alternative response:* "How do you expect to pay for this? It better not be coming out of my budget, or I'll go to the school board!"]

4. Professional Learning Communities are proposed. Your response:

    ☐ a. You volunteer to lead one and create the schedule.
    ☐ b. You hope you are put in your friend's group, as that will make it more palatable.
    ☐ c. "I'm not going—they can't make me attend this thing. I'm not volunteering for anything!"
    ☐ d. "I'll be there all right; someone's got to watch out for these new folks and be certain they don't change anything around here."

5. The new assistant principal of school counseling proposes a meeting to discuss a new way to build the master schedule and he puts a copy of the proposed method in your box. Your response:

    ☐ a. "Hmm, this sounds interesting; I think I'll read up on it so I can be of assistance."
    ☐ b. "Everyone seems to think this is a good idea; I guess I'll go along."
    ☐ c. "I'm not reading this stupid article, and I don't want to go to the meeting either. It's not my job to do scheduling; just give me my schedule."
    ☐ d. "Ha! They think they're going to change how we do it around here? Well, they've got another think coming. We've always done it this way, and we're not changing now. I'm scheduling a meeting to rally the others to put a stop to this!"

6. Your principal inquires about your counseling staff presenting developmental school counseling curriculum lessons in the classroom. Your response:

    ☐ a. You go online, download lessons, and propose them at the next meeting.
    ☐ b. You are glad your colleague will take care of this by going online to download the lessons.
    ☐ c. "I'm not presenting school counseling curriculum lessons, because I don't believe in it."
    ☐ d. "I'm going to put a stop to this lesson thing. I'll convince the teachers it's a waste of teaching time."

THE P³H FLIGHT TEST

7. **The staff wants to schedule a retreat to create a mission statement and establish yearly goals. Your response:**

    ☐ a. You clear your calendar because this will be fun!
    ☐ b. You'll bring a book in case it's boring.
    ☐ c. "I'm not going; we did this last year and it was a complete waste of time."
    ☐ d. "I'm going there to be certain they don't put in anything I don't agree with. We kept things out last time and we'll keep them out again."

8. **A researcher presents national data on equity and access issues at your school site. Your response:**

    ☐ a. You corral a team to look at site data.
    ☐ b. You attend a meeting on site data but do nothing.
    ☐ c. You avoid the meeting.
    ☐ d. You attend the meeting to ensure it does not lead to changes you don't approve of.

9. **A new principal asks you to join her to interview new teachers for the school. Your response:**

    ☐ a. "I'm glad she took me up on my offer to help interview—I hope we can find some really great passionate teachers!"
    ☐ b. "Since she asked me, I'll go this one time and see how I like it."
    ☐ c. "I don't want to go. I'll have to create substitute plans, the students will be out of control, and for what? We never get the teacher I want anyway."
    ☐ d. "You better believe I'm going! I only want teachers who think like I do in my department."

10. The assistant principal tells you he has to close the parking lot on your side of the school, because cars entering and leaving the lot will be a safety hazard for students going to the new portable classrooms on the other side of the lot. You think the plan is misguided. Your response:

    - ☐ a. You approach the administrator with an alternative plan and ask if there is any way it can be considered.
    - ☐ b. You do nothing, because you know the lead math teacher is dealing with it.
    - ☐ c. You go on stress leave for a week.
    - ☐ d. You remove the "No Parking" sign and park there anyway, because no one is going to tell *you* where to park.

11. The principal would like to create a new tardy policy. Your response:

    - ☐ a. You volunteer to be on the committee, as you have some great ideas.
    - ☐ b. You plan to follow the policy when it is created.
    - ☐ c. You grumble that this one won't work either, because they never work.
    - ☐ d. You attend the meeting and confront every idea presented or assumption made. [*Alternative response:* You don't attend, but when the new policy comes out, you tell others not to follow it, because this principal doesn't know what she is doing, and those people who created it are naïve.]

12. Your professional organization seeks to make major changes in its bylaws. Your response:

    - ☐ a. You volunteer to help with drafting the changes.
    - ☐ b. You agree to vote for the changes.
    - ☐ c. You don't belong to your professional association, because you couldn't care less.
    - ☐ d. You assume the bylaw changes will benefit only the executive director and her staff, so you rally others in an effort to stop the changes from being voted on by the membership.

FLIGHT TEST RESULTS

Regardless of whether you took the quiz with yourself or your team members/coworkers in mind, if you found your answers were mostly (a)'s, you or your coworkers are pilots; mostly (b)'s, passengers; (c)'s, prisoners; and (d)'s, hijackers. In making systemic change in schools, you need to be an expert on each role and how to identify those who fit these roles, as subsequent chapters will discuss.

I am a PILOT

Give me the map.

Tell me where to go and when to be there and I'll get you there.

I'll get us *all* there safely and on time.

2 Archetype Profiles

PILOTS

Pilots are leaders, advocates, and systems change agents. These are the individuals in an organization who seek to lead. They know what they (and the organization) need and are in the front of the plane, ready to move forward in the right direction, with their eyes on the horizon. They sign up first for conferences, come early, sit up front, and stay for the entire session. They know they have come for a reason and seek the information the training is providing—they come looking for a *map*. Pilots are the first people to the staff meetings; they also raise their hands, attend and engage, and offer to lead the team on the next project. Pilots have the confidence and competence necessary to move forward—they just need the opportunity and a map showing where they are headed. Pilots may or may not create their own maps; they either receive the map from the air traffic control tower or chart their own course. Either way, they are ready for take off.

Pilots want to be in charge; no, rather, they *need* to be in charge. They much prefer flying the plane themselves to allowing or trusting others to fly. Their value is wrapped up in making a difference, doing a good job and pleasing others. Pilots sometimes resent having to do everything, and they wish others would just put their hands on the control column and co-pilot the plane. But pilots are hesitant to delegate to others, because they are often let down. Pilots often have a group of passengers who appreciate all they do as a leader, but what the pilot really wishes is that the passengers would help more; however, the passengers might not do it *right*. This struggle produces a real quandary for the pilot.

> **WHAT DO PILOTS WANT?**
> They want to lead,
> be in control,
> make a difference,
> get credit,
> be appreciated for their skills,
> wear the nice uniform,
> be pointed out as "the captain,"
> and to get more good help.

P³H: PILOTS, PASSENGERS, PRISONERS & HIJACKERS

I am a PASSENGER

I come on time. I sit in my assigned seat.

I get up when asked and sit down when requested.

I enjoy the ride, the drinks, and the movie. I exit when the ride is over.

I expect the pilot to get me there safely and on time.

PASSENGERS

Passengers are "happy to be here." They are *thrilled* there is a pilot in charge. They have no interest in flying the plane but are eager to go along for the ride. While they might be able or willing to lead, they have no need to fly themselves right now. Passengers are glad someone else is willing to do more and they focus on doing only what is asked. They are centered with themselves and willing to do the required tasks, but no more. Passengers are content to do what they are asked, but they don't have a need or desire to go out of their way to please others. They may be teachers, counselors, or even assistant principals.

Much like children in the back seat of a car on a road trip, if passengers are fed, hydrated, and entertained, they are happy campers. They are less concerned about where they are going than they are being comfortable getting there, because they trust their pilots and know the pilot will have everyone's best interest at heart. They support the pilots, trust in their ability to fly the plane and are comfortable going along for the ride. Passengers know the pilot has the map (or believe they do) and relax in the comfort that all is well. They move forward behind the pilot in a supportive way.

Passengers are compliant, helpful, calm and patient team players, who believe they have an important, but not vital, role in the healthy environment of the school, district, or organization. They may appear to contribute by maintaining the status quo. They are the staple of the school, district, or organization: calm, cool, and collected. They do not ask many questions, and they usually don't panic when there is temporary turbulence. Passengers understand that turbulence is part of the ride and believe, know and trust pilots to do their best to ensure they will get to smoother air as soon as possible. In this same way, passengers in organizations trust the leaders, and learn to stay out of the way and do their jobs. They typically come on time, sit and stand when allowed, wait patiently when there are delays, and are loyal to their pilot; they will defend the pilot and the airline (school, district, organization) so long as they are treated well.

Passengers need to be treated respectfully, provided beverages, shown movies, and given blankets when cold and pillows when sleepy. For the most part, passengers rarely complain. They appreciate perks and recognize that sometimes tough times flying are just part of what they signed up for. Whether the plane moves fast or slow, or arrives early or late, the passengers tend to be polite and thankful to the pilots for landing them safely.

Passengers expect that most of time the ride will be smooth; and that the pilot will know what to do and when to do it, if trouble arises.

Passengers do not want to be at the helm or held responsible for the other passengers on board. They put themselves in the pilot's hands. They may consider the electronics of the pilot's gauges too complicated; when they do understand the gauges, they choose not to put in the effort to use the data the gauges provide.

Passengers tend to be well-adjusted people who have a life outside of work. Some are loyal and compliant followers who care about the mission of the work. For others, it's a job, but it is a job they do well. Their significant other, children, and hobbies are where they spend their time and their passion. They are stable bread-and-butter employees who can be trusted and depended upon.

Plenty of passengers are former pilots who grew tired of all the pressure in the cockpit. A pilot's role is stressful; there is a tremendous amount of responsibility. If the pilot crashes the plane, people die. If the president of a company goes bankrupt, hundreds or thousands of employees might be out of work and not fed. A pilot chooses to take on this level of authority; a passenger does not.

WHAT DO PASSENGERS WANT?

They want to come on time, do their work, take their lunch break, and be left alone and trusted to do their jobs.

They are not interested in personal relationships with their pilots outside of work.

They are comfortable being part of the movement forward, just *not* being in charge of it.

They want to get where they are going, and it is okay with them if someone else heads.

They are more than happy to support the leader.

ARCHETYPE PROFILES

I am a PRISONER

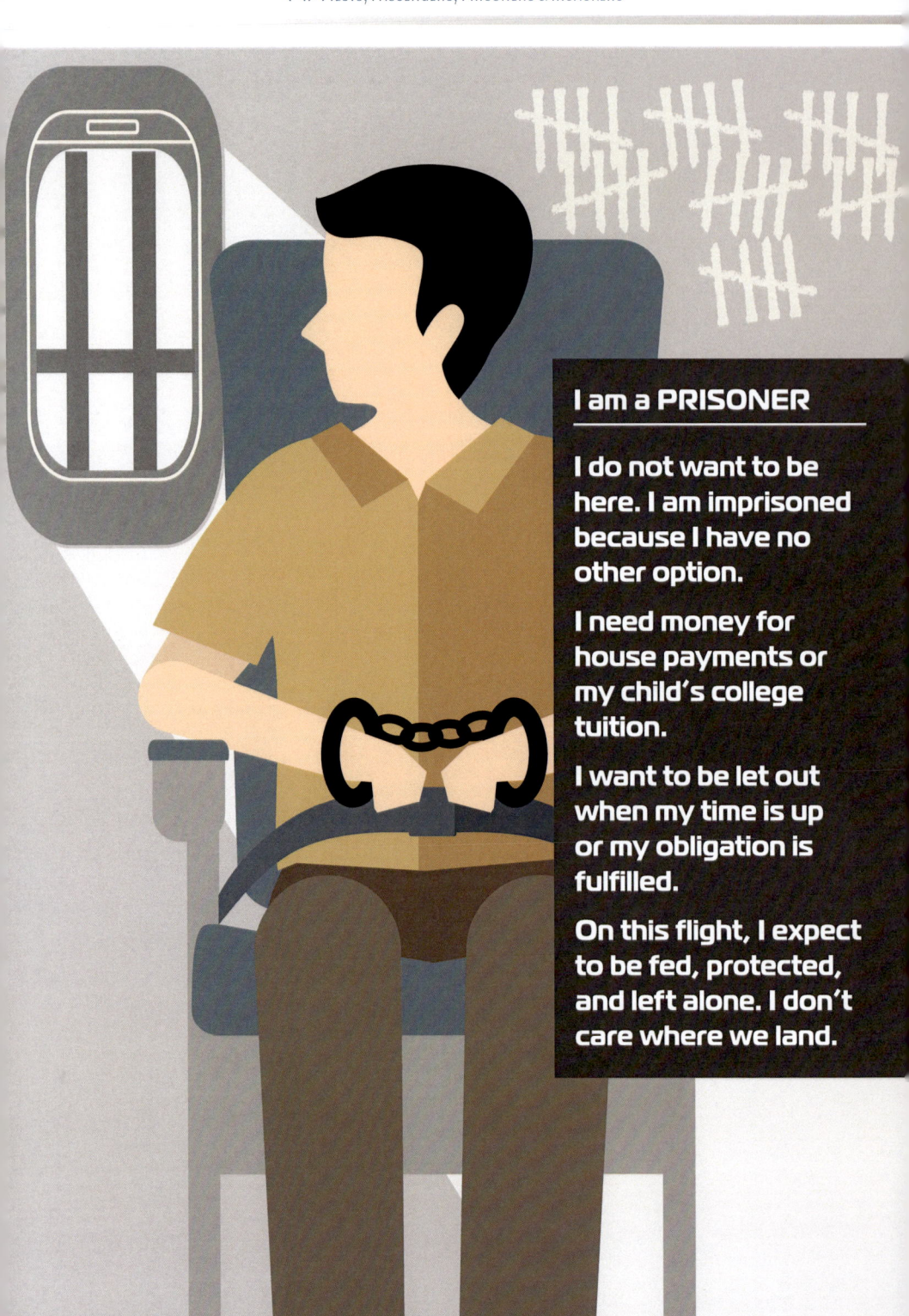

I do not want to be here. I am imprisoned because I have no other option.

I need money for house payments or my child's college tuition.

I want to be let out when my time is up or my obligation is fulfilled.

On this flight, I expect to be fed, protected, and left alone. I don't care where we land.

PRISONERS

Prisoners are on the plane, but they do not want to be there. They want off the plane. They are ready to retire, wish they could quit, and are just doing their time. They may have once entered the profession because they loved the career, but that has now changed. They are chained to the job by their need for income or fear of leaving. They are grumblers who are tired and burned out. They may have been passengers (or even pilots) years ago, but they have been on the plane way too long. They complain about everything; but, if treated nicely, tend to respond more like passengers. Prisoners did not choose this flight (or this training, organizational leader, school, etc.) but somehow are stuck here.

Disgruntled tenured teachers, counselors, or administrators who hate teaching, the students, or new technology are prime examples. The job has changed but they have not. One to five years from retirement and clearly frustrated with the school system, the pilots, and everyone around them, prisoners complain at staff meetings, grumble that "We tried that before and it didn't work," and are naysayers to those who support change efforts. Prisoners are annoying but usually harmless (as long as they are handcuffed by their reasons for being on the job), but, given too much voice, they can be dangerous to morale and the forward progress of the system. Prisoners are typically not so angry that they'd crash the plane; instead, they make life uncomfortable for everyone else. They are not invested in the work, the people, or the career. Prisoners are handcuffed to the salary and benefits.

WHAT DO PRISONERS WANT?

They want to get *out*.
They're miserable.
They are tired, spent and burned out.
They don't care to go to new places, they want to get off the plane. Unfortunately, they are chained to it and can't move.
They are in a rut, entrenched and unhappy.
They are *defiantly* upset.

P³H: PILOTS, PASSENGERS, PRISONERS & HIJACKERS

~~Pilot's Plan~~

My Plan

I am a HIJACKER

I have my own map and my own agenda.

I will go my own way and I will not share it with you.

No one will take me in a direction I do not want to go. If they try to, I will destroy them *and* their mission.

I'll get us all where *I* want to go, on *my* schedule. Safety and time are no factor.

HIJACKERS

Hijackers take all of this very seriously; *someone* has to! Hijackers believe they know what is best and the people in charge know nothing. They believe that if only the management would listen to them, things would be better; but since no one does, their mission is to ensure nothing happens that might take the plane anywhere but where they want it to go.

Hijackers are the employees that organizational leaders must watch out for. They want you to take the plane where *they* choose (never where the pilot intends), as they would rather see the plane crash and burn than go where they don't want it to go. Hijackers are negative leaders who have their *own* agenda and are utilizing the vehicle of the school, district, or organization to drive that agenda. Hijackers are dangerous because they have no concern for the well-being of others and no care for the plane's intended destination. They believe so deeply that what they are doing is in the best interests of others that the end justifies the means. To hijackers, this is war and collateral damage occurs albeit with innocent victims. They board the plane with the full intention of hijacking it to their chosen route, regardless of whether the pilot agrees, or harm is caused on the way.

Hijackers can be found in any compartment of the airplane; they may even be in the cockpit (the most dangerous position of all). Hijackers are often disguised as one of the other archetypes. They rarely announce themselves as hijackers, and no label exists to notify or warn you in advance of who they are. They might appear to be compliant passengers or a quiet teacher who, in actuality, is a hijacker behind the scenes. Worse yet, they might be in the cockpit, sitting beside the pilot, waiting for the perfect opportunity to take over the plane. Knowledge is power and to hijackers, learning about the pilot, the aircraft, and other passengers, is essential before deciding when to hijack the plane in their direction.

WHAT DO HIJACKERS WANT?

They want to be pilots.
They want to be in control, but they are not.
So they seek to destroy those who are in charge, take them down, change the direction of the plane, or destroy it completely.

PILOT'S LOG

You know, I hadn't thought of it before, but when I need to add a student to a class that is already full, I always pick a class where the teacher is a pilot. These teachers always say, "Sure! Put the student in my class—the child can use my chair until we get another one!" If the class of a pilot isn't available, I choose a passenger's class, but I avoid asking favors from prisoners or hijackers. I'd rather put the new student in the wrong class with a pilot than in the correct class with a hijacker.

—**Sylvia,** *School Counselor*

FLIGHT STATUS

Smooth Air	Action Taken
When pilots don't see a problem	they maintain and monitor the flight for the best performance.
When passengers don't see a problem	they do what's expected of them and enjoy the flight.
When prisoners don't see a problem	they are indifferent but less difficult to work with.
When hijackers don't see a problem	they take advantage of the calm to plot their next move.

Turbulence	Action Taken
When pilots see a problem	they jump in and help out.
When passengers see a problem	they look around to see who will help. If asked, they will help.
When prisoners see a problem	they are not willing to help. It is not their problem.
When hijackers see a problem	they sit back and grin and enjoy the chaos. They may, in fact, have caused the problem.

II
Working With Your Fellow Flyers

This section provides recommendations for those seeking ways to work more effectively with each of the four archetypes. Included are examples of each archetype and comments from professional educators who have attended my trainings and conference sessions on handling difficult colleagues.

3 Flying With Pilots

WHAT PILOTS HAVE TO OFFER

There are many advantages to being a *pilot*; they are energetic, enthusiastic and eager to do well. They are engaged learners who love to learn new things and they thrive on the knowledge and ideas designed to make things better within the organization. Pilots support others. They are often willing to help fellow staff members when others won't. They go out on a limb to assist others and can be counted on to be supportive of those in need. They are loyal to the organization and make confident leaders. They are great mentors to those seeking to be copilots and receive joy from seeing their mentees become pilots themselves.

There are also disadvantages in being a *pilot*. Pilots run the risk of going more than one direction at once when they have too many good ideas. They rarely say no to others and may not take good care of themselves. Consequently, pilots can spend so much energy flying they are prone to burning out. It is interesting that pilots love to get credit for their work, which is not a negative; except when they take *all* the credit. They are pilots because their needs are met by the reinforcement of others. When praise is not forthcoming, they may be hurt by the lack of recognition, especially if another takes credit for their work. If their integrity is challenged, they may be devastated. After all, they have devoted their lives to this work, project, school, district, and/or organization, and to be questioned can deeply distress them.

Pilots are occasionally discouraged by those they expected to help them lead, but let them down instead. They often assume that their passengers will have telepathic knowledge of what needs to be done next, and that they will step in and copilot without direction. When this does not occur, pilots may become disappointed. They believe, that since they can see the flight path clearly, others should see it as well. They might wonder, "How is it that Employee X doesn't recognize *this* is the training we need? It is so obvious to me!" Further, they may resent others who do not lead as much or as well as they expect. If they become too discouraged, they may become hijackers (negative leaders).

STRATEGIES FOR WORKING WITH PILOTS

Let Them Lead, and Then Get Out of Their Way
Pilots like being in charge. While they will tell you they want help with projects, often they would simply prefer to do the work alone so they can control the outcome. They also, however, like to have reassurance that they are headed in a generally approved direction. Recognizing when they want help, or prefer to do it by themselves, is an important skill.

You may find clues to this when they are seeking input, feedback, or criticism. Perhaps they are only seeking your reflections on the progress of their work, not actually share in the decision-making. Instead of giving them your preference when they provide options, consider replying that they have presented interesting ideas and then inquire what they think is the best way to go. (What would they recommend?) You can support pilots in this way, whether you are their supervisor, a copilot in their school, or a passenger under their supervision.

Give Them the Credit They Deserve
As mentioned earlier, the spirit of a pilot is fed by their success. Pilots thrive on positive reinforcement. If they earn praise, deliver it. Some pilots will appear somewhat embarrassed by all the attention, but no matter—inside, they are delighted with it. Nothing hurts a pilot more than having gone above and beyond to ensure a task was completed, only to be treated as if it were an expectation. Perhaps it was, but pilots feel hurt if they are not appreciated for the time and effort they took to complete a task.

> It's hard for me sometimes when others just expect I will do something. For instance, I have always completed this major project [building the master schedule] in the summer without help. I work on it until the wee hours of the morning, and sometimes I miss out sometimes on family events, vacation, etc. Instead of thanking me, sometimes a prisoner boss will criticize my work, or a pilot boss will take all the credit and I am left fuming. It makes me want to think about becoming a hijacker. I prefer being a pilot, but I just need a little more appreciation.
>
> —**Russell,** *High School Assistant Principal*

Appreciate Their Skills
Acknowledge a pilot's skills in certain areas—their egos need to be stroked in this way, but be authentic, they'll see right through your façade if you don't mean what you say. One way to show appreciation is to *ask them to mentor you*. Pilots love to bring copilots into the cockpit and teach them the ropes. If you are interested in becoming a pilot, let them know.

They'll also get the message that they're appreciated if occasionally, you *remind them to take care of themselves*. Pilots are bad at taking care of themselves. They will suggest others go home on time and then stay late alone to finish a project. Reminding pilots to take time for themselves lets them know you care about them.

Encourage Them to Give the Credit Away
When pilots are moving forward (often too quickly) they may overlook the importance of giving credit where credit is due. Whenever various school or district recognitions or awards are given out, they often go to the leader, when the truth is, successes are often the result of a team effort. When pilots allow others to take credit—by taking a step back and giving the credit away to the team—they demonstrate much needed humility and share recognition with those who may have been overlooked.

My longtime mentor and brother told me: "Trish, give it away—let someone else take credit for it. It will come back to you tenfold." It was a difficult lesson to learn at first, but he is absolutely right. Giving credit away to others encourages them to do the same. It does come back.

Remind Them to Wait for the Passengers to Come on Board
One of the best ways to help pilots is to let them know when they are going so fast that others are being left behind. They are probably unaware of this, and they would be more than willing to slow down if enlightened. Remind them politely, to wait for the others to come on board before taking off, because a solid passenger base is important.

Pssst—sometimes give the credit away.
...and we couldn't have done it without your hard work...
Humility—that's a rare quality these days.

Frequent Flyer

Jasmine is a natural-born pilot. She sees the destination and almost doesn't need a map—she flies with her gut and instincts, and she's on target. Jasmine is an advocate for equity and access for students who have been underrepresented. She defends and protects all students' rights to rigorous course work. She herds 10th grade students into her AP psychology course like cattle and then does an amazing thing: She ensures they *are* successful. She does whatever it takes to assist, mentor, support, defend—and occasionally browbeat—her students, and they are successful. Her students *pass* the college level courses (even though the hijackers in the teacher's lounge believe they can't), because she doesn't tell them they are average or below average students. Instead, she tells them they *can*, and they *do*.

Jasmine is a young, passionate, headstrong pilot who is as excited about her opportunities to teach as she is frustrated with the systems that hinder her and the prisoner and hijacking teachers who challenge the direction she flies in. Her area of growth as a pilot is to ensure she doesn't fly the plane so fast that others can't keep up, or passengers become frightened. The concern is if she speeds up too fast, she may take off before others have even boarded the plane. What good is it if she flies to the destination alone? It is vital that the pilot have an air of confidence, assurance, and vision when flying, but being too excited and too zealous—having too much energy—can cause passengers to be nervous about her flying abilities.

Imagine you are on a plane, and the pilot repeatedly uses the intercom to point out each landmark along the way. What are your thoughts? First, I'd wonder: *Hasn't she flown here before? Is this her first time?* Or maybe: *Why does she feel the need to share all this with me? If I wanted to know, I'd look out the window myself and read the map! Leave me alone and let me vegetate here! I'm trying to sleep and you are waking me up!* Or worse, I might think: *Who's flying the plane when you are busy pointing these things out to me?* I'd wonder how the pilot could do both well and rather the pilot just concentrated on flying the plane!

So Jasmine (as department chair) is a great pilot for her small fleet of social studies teachers. She is part of the fleet of small planes and she is a copilot on the larger plane (the school plane). Jasmine is so good, other pilots are encouraging her to become the pilot of a larger plane (principal). But she is not interested; she likes the control she has in a small plane.

4 Flying With Passengers

WHAT PASSENGERS HAVE TO OFFER

While pilots seek to lead, *passengers* appreciate the fact that someone *else* is in charge. Passengers are wonderfully supportive members of a staff or organization. They are agreeable and typically support pilots, because they are glad someone else is flying the plane. Passengers *follow*. If they really trust the pilot, they do not question the direction; rather, they assume the pilot has everything under control.

By and large, 80% of the staff are passengers They are the caretakers of the children, the keepers of the dream, the dutiful implementers and loyal employees. Without passengers, there is no school. They are the new teachers and counselors trying to figure it out, wanting to learn and trying to follow, hoping to neither let the pilot down nor be let down themselves. They are moms and dads who are extremely compliant and who avoid over-committing to balance work and family obligations. Being a passenger is an honorable, worthy and esteemed role. Without passengers, there are no pilots.

One concern pilots often have with passengers is that they seem to lack the pilot's level of passion and commitment. Passengers are passive supporters and they will not step up unless specifically asked for help. They rarely volunteer without incentives (free round-trip ticket, anyone?) and some never step up even when incentives are offered. (I once was on an overbooked plane with 200 people and *no one* took the airline incentive.)

Much like those on United Airlines flight 93 on 9/11, passengers can and do rise to the role of pilot when the situation calls for drastic action. Once the danger is averted, however, they return to their passenger roles, although they remain alert to any potential disasters. Passengers do not openly complain or advocate; however, they are the ones who, in an effort to support and protect their pilot, will quietly walk into the principal's office, close the door and say, "I just need you to know...." They trust and appreciate their pilot and will do what it takes to make sure the pilot is protected.

Passengers are the silent supporters who, just like students, pass through high school unnoticed, shuffling through their entire careers without getting their names in the local paper or receiving awards for leading teams to the finals of mock trial. They are the cattle and the sheep—they want to be respected as professionals but not asked to do one more thing. If you respect them, they'll have your back and support you to the nth degree. If you push them too hard, they will become prisoners—or worse—hijackers.

> **Frequent Flyer**
>
> Attacking the integrity of a pilot is one of the hijacker's greatest weapons, as hijackers recognize the core *need* of great pilots to keep their integrity intact. Pilots lead by example and are respected for their abilities. Hijackers undermine pilots by manipulating their followers with menacing intent. For example, they may spread inaccurate rumors among faculty about the intentions of a new policy or practice they disagree with, thereby undermining not only forward progress but the reputation of a pilot who advocates for the innovation. This can alter the career path of a new pilot whose skin is not thick enough to successfully depersonalize the action of the hijacker. Instead, a pilot may decide that being a passenger is just fine after all.
>
> **Andrew was** one such pilot. A school counselor early in his career, he was later tapped for administration. Schooled and confident, Andrew put himself out to the wolves when he worked for a principal so awful the district eventually fired the principal, rather than move him to another school (a rare event), but not before he had done a lot of damage. During those years, this principal—a hijacker in the pilot's seat—professionally destroyed his copilots: None of his assistant principals stayed in administration. The hijacker principal's tactic was to blame his errors on the others and attack both their credibility and integrity with the staff and district office alike. Andrew wasn't savvy enough to recognize the hijacker in the pilot seat. Unable to recover, he chose to return to the school counseling ranks, where he would ride out the rest of his career as a passenger.

STRATEGIES FOR WORKING WITH PASSENGERS

Celebrate Successes

Passengers probably won't be the coaches of the state's winning mock trial team, because that's too much work—these folks don't go above and beyond to earn the type of adulation that gets in the newspaper. Nonetheless, their contributions should be appreciated. If achievement scores are up in their class, then celebrate it. Think of them as the students who plug away every day. We pay more attention to those that do well or get into trouble. Passengers often go underappreciated. Find time to share their successes.

Praise them publicly: Don't go overboard, but (in this case) a public display of professional affirmation is okay and appreciated.

> I am a passenger, but sometimes I feel more like a prisoner. I try to change what I teach. I ask for a new class—I switch from algebra to geometry, or try an honors class just to shake it up. I don't want to be a prisoner. I have seen too many of my colleagues unhappy. So I try to notice when I start to resent the students or the work. I tell my department chair that I want to put in for new classes just to stay stimulated and hopefully, not turn into a prisoner. I know I'll never be a pilot, but I'd like to stay a passenger.
>
> –Richard, *High School Teacher*

Recognize Small Daily Contributions

Don't wait for the huge victory; recognize any movement in the right direction.

Thank them for being on time. It may seem trite, but because passengers typically already do the "right thing," they are rarely appreciated for it. Instead, people just assume they will do the right thing, but passengers should be thanked just like anyone else. It lets them know others notice and care. It builds allegiance. Ever notice how flight attendants do this as passengers exit an airplane? "Thank you for coming." "Thanks folks." "See you next time." "Drive safely."

Thank them for picking up after themselves. Passengers require little support, feedback, or energy; therefore thanking them for small things goes a long way. This takes little time and they are typically the folks that value order in their lives. Appreciating it helps maintain it.

Thank them for attending open house. Not attending open house is typically not an option at most school sites; however, there are always some staff who don't attend. Passengers know that usually nothing happens to those who don't attend—after all, it's not a severe enough offense to fire someone, it's just a frustrating sign of noncompliance. Appreciating those passengers who do attend open house, sets a good tone.

Enlist Their Support and Cooperation

Passengers are a good source of support for school initiatives, and their help can be enlisted without requiring a lot of the passion or commitment that they don't have. Typically, they must be invited or asked to show support; therefore, enlisting their cooperation on an activity is important. Don't assume they will see it as important. Remember, their motivation isn't tied to success; they will not see the same value in things. Ask them specifically to help and do it individually, as group requests for help will be ignored. Most likely they will be happy to do it, but if you wait for them to think of it, you may be left frustrated.

When you ask for support, be sure to provide *plenty of time and assistance*, because passengers may feel overwhelmed if rushed. If you assign an important task to a passenger, remember to follow up regularly if you want it completed on time. Remember, the task is your agenda, not theirs.

Utilize them for consensus on important topics. Because they would rather please you than invest in the issue at hand, it is helpful to enlist passengers for opportunities where they can help provide consensus on an important topic or issue. Perhaps you want to try a new bell schedule. You are well prepared for the prisoners and hijackers who will resist and you know the copilots are on board. If you enlist a few passengers and explain to them why it is necessary, they may also decide to support you (even if they really don't care about the new schedule), simply because you asked.

Put them on committees where voting—not action or work—matters. The issue here is if you put them on a committee where the action that takes place is not of value—they will soon become prisoners. Only on those committees where voting matters is it beneficial to enlist passengers to counterbalance possible prisoners and hijackers.

Remember Passengers Have Two Lives

Passengers have a life at school. The also have a life *out* of school. They may love both, but prioritize home over school. These folks are typically invested in activities with their families over activities with workmates outside of work. Since they aren't internally motivated by a need for personal validation, they are ok with not attending staff happy hour events, Saturday night card games, or the Sunday Major League Baseball game. Therefore, don't push too hard for out-of-work relationships. Consider building and maintaining positive, professional relationships, rather than pushing for personal ones.

SCHOOL PROGRESS COMMITTEE
OK, let's vote.
How many in favor?
Raise your hands.
The committee needs my vote to break the tie.

Look Out for Hidden Pilots

Even though most passengers just want to stay on autopilot, within their ranks are hidden pilots who need only to be tapped for a leadership role. These are the staff members who need just the slightest amount of encouragement—they might have the abilities and potential but have never been offered the opportunity—who will emerge during trainings, retreats and trying times. Look out during these moments for copilots, they are often the best ones you'll have.

> **Frequent Flyer**
>
> **Jordan was a passenger for 30 years.** She stayed in the shadows until it became clear the school was in crisis, and then she spoke up. Having been in the school 30 years, when she noticed the school was in trouble, she stepped up to the front of the plane and addressed the staff. Her voice was heard and they trusted her, because she had not made a habit of speaking out. Had she been at the podium every year as a cheerleader copilot, no one would have listened. If she had used the podium every year with a complaint (as a prisoner), they wouldn't have listened either; and if she had been a hijacker, she wouldn't have lasted 30 years. Jordan was a passenger—a hard-working, trusting, caring, dedicated passenger who did her job but chose not to lead. However, when the school fell apart, she could take it no longer. Recognizing the principal was a hijacker and more copilots were needed to diffuse the situation, Jordan stepped up, stepped in, became a pilot momentarily, and was *heard*. After the crisis was over (and the principal fired) Jordan went respectfully back to her classroom. She still comes to meetings, but she sits quietly and supports the leaders she trusts.

5 Flying With Prisoners

WHAT PRISONERS HAVE TO OFFER

There are some advantages to having a few *prisoners* on staff. Prisoners require the use of people-friendly facilitation skills. If you appear arrogant, self-centered, or cocky, a passenger may never tell you, but a prisoner will—they tell the truth when others (passengers and hijackers) don't. Prisoners are brutally honest and have no discomfort sharing their frustration with you, the system, or the world. But it's interesting, because if you do manage to win over prisoners and gain their allegiance, they may become your greatest supporters. Under all that complaining, prisoners do not feel vengeful but rather disenfranchised, and they may respond well to your compassion.

While one or two prisoners might keep you on your toes, having too many can disrupt your flight. Their constant complaints and negative attitudes can change the momentum of any forward progress. When new ideas or the opportunity to take new approaches arise, prisoners are the first ones to assume it won't work, because these ideas "have never worked and never will." This negativity makes the ride less comfortable for everyone. Prisoners are high-maintenance and require a tremendous amount of patience to manage them well.

> **Frequent Flyer**
>
> **George is a prisoner.** He's finished. He's "over it" and wishes he could quit, but his kids are in college and he needs the income. And since he's unhappy, others should be too. George blames everyone else for everything wrong in the school. Whether it's the students' problems or the administrator's problem, it certainly isn't his problem. He doesn't need help, mentoring, additional training, a conference to learn new skills, or any suggestions on how to improve his teaching. He knows all he plans to know and is biding his time, complaining about everything, and hoping to retire one day soon. Any attempt to assist only upsets him, because it implies that he has a problem, which he certainly *does not*.

STRATEGIES FOR WORKING WITH PRISONERS

Don't take their gruff mood or satirical off-the-cuff remarks personally. It's not that prisoners want to do a bad job or hurt kids, they just don't see any way out. Complaining about prisoners only perpetuates negative attitudes in a school, district, or organization.

The keys to working with prisoners are *respect and compassion*. Remember they are *hurting*. They would leave if they could, but they can't. They are chained to the job (it is no longer a satisfying career for them), because they need the money, benefits, etc. Typically, their attitude is a result of years of disenfranchisement. It will help to remember that they have been hurt for some time and may once have been young eager idealists. The world has changed, but they have not.

Show Respect

Listen to them when they want to talk. Prisoners are disenfranchised. Requiring them to wait to be heard contributes to their frustration. Rather than schedule an appointment to meet with them, take time to meet when they ask, even if only for a minute. Remember, with the prisoner, it is usually not you they are upset with—it is the system. Rather than adding yourself to the list of those they are upset with, meet with them as soon as possible, and validate their fears, worries, and concerns. Often, good listening will diffuse their concerns to resolve the issue.

Never agree with others that they are prisoners. You know they are prisoners, but keep it quiet. When others suggest it, do not agree that Mr. or Mrs. So-and-So should retire. It perpetuates the reality of their disenfranchisement. Instead, portray prisoners as good people who are struggling.

Demonstrate Compassion

Be polite and friendly. Say hello to them, let them know you care, appreciate their predicament and will treat them kindly. Avoid the temptation to pick on them or whisper that they are old and should retire. Perhaps other staff will follow your lead and be more compassionate as well. Compassion breeds more compassion and it is hard to stay angry when people are nice to you. Besides, when prisoners are less angry, they are easier to be around.

Make them as comfortable as possible. They are already upset with the world; why add to their discomfort? Remember they don't want to be in your school any more than you want them there. See what you can do to make their lives easier—give them all morning classes, or a classroom near the parking lot. They will leave early anyway, but forcing them to walk across campus puts them in unnecessary contact with others they can complain to. Why ruin anyone else's day? Let them get in and out and leave everyone else alone. Their comfort results in less discontent for all.

Help them get through the day without a crisis. If you know it will be a bad day for a prisoner (you know they are meeting with a potentially difficult parent or guardian, for example), check in and offer to assist. Letting prisoners know you are there provides a foundation of support. Also, helping them get through the day helps you get through the day.

> I remember being incredibly angry and frustrated with "prisoners" when I first started working. I couldn't understand why they were in the profession if they hated it so much. I was young and passionate and full of ideas and they shot me down every time. At least I was smart enough not to say anything, because then I would have turned them against me and I didn't need that when I was just starting out.
>
> –**Amanda,** Middle School Counselor

Enlist Their Support; Then Value Their Contributions

Don't tell them to do anything—make a request and enlist their support. Prisoners rarely respond to demands, but when they do, they comply with resistance and grumbling. Enlisting their support, however, while they may not seem eager, cuts through the power trip and produces staff members who are more likely to perform requested tasks.

Look for and recognize good days. We all have bad days, and while prisoners tend to have more, there will also be good days. Noticing, acknowledging and appreciating the good days and the various successes that occur from time to time, may contribute to feelings of empowerment, which may, in turn, increase the opportunities for even more good days.

P³H: PILOTS, PASSENGERS, PRISONERS & HIJACKERS

> I want to discuss a new opportunity where your talents are much needed.

PRINCIPAL

Appreciate any contribution. In the case of a prisoner, the contribution may be the lack of complaints, but whatever the contribution, find a way to appreciate it.

Help Them Recognize That You Are Not the Enemy

Remember: You are not their captor; their contract is. It is not your problem that they are here or unhappy—it is theirs. They chose this profession and they are responsible for that decision. Because you are not their captor, *they have their own keys to their own handcuffs,* and they can unlock them if and when they choose to do so.

Put a surprise in their box. There is value in practicing random acts of kindness—especially for prisoners who have given up on anyone caring about them. Since they will most likely choose to not participate in the "secret pal" or "secret Santa" club, where faculty members exchange gifts, surprise them anyway—make their day (anonymously).

Bring them things from conferences. It is funny what gifts, even little ones, can do. Once I went to a conference and brought back bags full of different freebees that I had picked up at the marketing tables. I placed them all on a table at a staff meeting, and asked everyone to line up and take one thing they wanted. It was amazing—even the prisoners pushed and shoved their way into line to get first crack at the goodies.

Offer to transfer them. It is a good idea to offer prisoners a transfer into another jail (school, district position, organization committee, or staff position). A change of scenery can bring them out of a depressive mood for a while. Sometimes just the physical change itself can provide them a honeymoon period. It is also wise to offer a one-for-one prisoner exchange, so that two parties will benefit from a change of pace.

Offer to help them with a new opportunity. If you think it would be best for the students or the school, district, or organization as a whole, help find them a new position. Perhaps they are in the wrong niche; a move to a different grade level or from one type of program to another can bring out their gifts in a new way and perhaps bring about the birth of a happy passenger.

PILOT'S LOG

Hannah hated her job as a second grade teacher. She was talented as a reading instructor, but had few skills in behavior management. While she could successfully teach a few students in a small group, others in the classroom were climbing on chairs, running about, and acting out of control. Hannah was miserable. She felt like a failure, hated coming to school, and wanted to quit, but she had no other career option. She was stuck with a mortgage and needed the work. Hannah needed a way out. I listened to her, empathized with her frustration, and tried to help her debrief some days as needed. One day, I asked Hannah if she had heard of the reading specialist position. The truth is, she was able to work with five or so kids at a time, but she struggled with a class of 30. So I suggested the reading specialist position to her as a solution, offered to write a letter of recommendation and encouraged her to apply. She soon applied and got the job, and it was a win-win solution. She was happier and the students were better off. Sometimes a prisoner needs to be given a pardon and a chance to contribute again.

–**Trish,** *Elementary School Counselor*

6 Flying With Hijackers

WHAT HIJACKERS HAVE TO OFFER

Ideally, there would be no *hijackers*, but truthfully, it is hard to imagine a school, district, or professional organization without them. On the positive side, hijackers keep pilots on their toes, as they require pilots to defend themselves and provide reasons for what they do and why they do it. The mere presence of hijackers forces pilots to create allegiances and alliances and not act independently.

Since they will be watching you (your mistakes are their playground), hijackers require others to always do the right thing. If you maintain your integrity in the face of a hijacker, then you are beyond reproach.

Not surprisingly, there are several disadvantages to having one or more hijackers on your staff. They can (and will attempt to) undermine and ruin a new, inexperienced administrator. This is why in many circumstances, when new or less seasoned administrators take over a school, the central office will offer them the opportunity to "involuntarily transfer" a few people on staff. If there are too many hijackers, administrators will fail before they have the time to garner allegiances among other pilots and passengers.

The trouble is, hijackers are often hard to identify. In fact, they might appear to be copilots or passengers. They might initially appear to be allies; engaging others in friendly, supportive, interactions and building trust. But no sooner will they engender your trust than they will use it against you. The important thing to remember about hijackers is that they want to publicly humiliate you, even if it makes them look bad as well. The victory for hijackers is not that they win—it is that *you* lose.

> **Frequent Flyer**
>
> **Mick was a hijacker.** On the surface he was quiet, respectful and polite; but privately, he was hijacking. He was not a prisoner, because he wasn't satisfied to just complain; rather, he acted with malice, such as the time he sent secret emails to the school board undermining the site administrators, who were never quite certain who the mole was in their midst.

STRATEGIES FOR WORKING WITH HIJACKERS

Hijackers are problematic, but they are part of the school family and therefore the first attempt to work with hijackers must be to embrace them with the strong hope of change. If reasonable attempts to address their hijacking behaviors fail, then other measures must be taken.

Know Your Hijackers
Getting to know your hijackers is vital.

Know who they hang out with. Since these folks may be the hijacker's moles in the school, district, or organization, it is good to know who they are and plan conversations accordingly.

Get to know their daily routines. Predicting hijacker's behavior is important, because if you know what their routine is, you can plan your day accordingly—in or out of their arena.

Imagine the world from their point of view. There will be times when you will wonder, "Where the hell are they coming from?" Try to assume good intentions, first. Attempt to be genuinely empathetic with the hijacker and put yourself in the hijacker's shoes. Use this understanding to predict the hijacker's actions. Imagine the behavior that may follow from their worldview and determine your options for action accordingly.

Use Praise to Minimize Their Power
Hijackers are self-centered and potentially malicious. While initially you might take their attacks personally, remember that their issues never were—and never will be—about you. However, they will try to *use* you, however hoping you will believe that their issues are about you. They will also attack you to gain power. Ironically, you can minimize their power by treating them the opposite way that they treat you.

Look for an area of strength and praise them publicly. The last thing hijackers will expect, is that you would praise or bolster them, especially if they believe you are out to get them as much as they are out to get you. Rising above the hijacker's counterproductive behavior sets an example of good leadership and can be a powerful tool.

Appreciate their smallest steps in any direction (unless it is backward). There is no reason to believe these individuals will ever act in an intentionally positive way, so appreciate steps—even to the side—as a form of change. Also, since you would voice appreciation for positive action by others, not appreciating their actions might tip them off that you are afraid of them.

Never badmouth them—ever. It is never acceptable to badmouth a hijacker. It tarnishes your reputation in the eyes of the other pilots and passengers, and for those who are trying to find your weaknesses, it becomes an indicator of your true colors. It plays your hand and lets everyone know how you feel. Remember, power is gained by not letting hijackers ever know they got to you. If you badmouth them, it is evident to them and anyone who hears you that your armor is defective.

Send a seasonal card (birthday or other special occasion). Why *not?* You are a nice person, and this is nice thing to do. More importantly, if you are sending others special occasion cards and you leave hijackers out, they will find out and it will be evident (to them) that they frighten, intimidate, or alarm you.

Do What They Least Expect

Stop by unexpectedly. If you are having a particularly confident day, stop by a hijacker's classroom, just to say "Hi!" This way, *you* are in control and the hijacker knows that you are not in any way intimidated or afraid. Enter the hijacker's turf on your terms.

Ignore negative behavior. This is especially true if it is directed at you. Become "Teflon" to criticism. Remove the opportunity for the hijacker to get the much-sought-after reaction.

Avoid confrontation. Arguments with hijackers won't work, because engagement in confrontation or arguing is a win for them and a loss for you.

Bring them in, closer. "The Godfather" had a quote: "Keep your friends close, keep your enemies closer."

Manage Your Meetings

Promise yourself that you will personally schedule and control all meetings with hijackers; this includes the setting, seating arrangements and time. To maintain control, it is imperative you meet with them only on *your* terms.

An unexpected visit means she's not intimidated.
Thought I'd stop in to see how things were going.
Keep your friends close and your enemies closer.

So if they come by your office, make it a point to be on your way somewhere and tell them, "I am so sorry, I'd love to meet with you, but I am on my way to _____. Is _____ a good time for you?" Have a plan in place for all meetings with hijackers—whether planned or unplanned.

Meetings with hijackers are inevitably difficult. To prepare, practice these potentially difficult conversations with others you trust. Determine courses of action and test-drive them on trusted colleagues. Their feedback will hone your skills and provide confidence when the actual event occurs. Role-play several possible outcomes and have a plan to address each one, making sure to include the worst-case scenario. When your colleagues know you have not placed all your bets on one hand, they are more likely to provide support, because they know you are committed to an action and have alternative plans to ensure its success.

Never accept impromptu meetings with hijackers. If you *do* accept an unplanned meeting, you are doing so on their terms. Teach your secretary or nearby allies to let you know if a hijacker is coming in your direction, or to inform the hijacker that you are unavailable. You must commit to yourself that you are *never* available for them on an impromptu basis. Make an arrangement with your secretary to interrupt you if you ever *do* accidentally find yourself in an unexpected meeting with a hijacker, so you can close it down if you need it.

Avoid meeting with them when you are sick, tired, upset, or vulnerable. If you meet with a hijacker during these times, the likelihood you will make a mistake is too great. Excuse yourself, apologize for rescheduling and meet only when you are certain of your skills and abilities to manage the situation.

Take copious notes after meetings with them. This is a must! Good records will protect you. If you don't keep records, inevitably the contents of a conversation will revisit you differently than you recall them—hijackers can twist your words into forms and meanings you neither meant nor even imagined. Trust me, there may be a day in court with hijackers—you will want to be prepared. So, document, *document,* DOCUMENT.

Always debrief with others after meeting with hijackers to keep yourself in check. These will often be somewhat stressful meetings. Having a trusted colleague available to debrief with you (preferably someone who knows you well and will provide *honest* feedback) can help you learn and gain strength from each experience.

Never play your full hand. Just let them *think* you have. Use self-disclosure sparingly and in a timely way. Share part of a personal story or professional event that you can control the message of. Perhaps you know a person who is retiring, but don't tell the hijacker that you have been selected for the position. This is a hard thing to do, but it's very important. Keeping some information to yourself ensures you have power in the relationship.

Use Active Listening Skills

Active listening skills reflect a hijacker's personal feelings and thoughts back to them. This may sound too easy, but it *works*. If hijackers complain that the in-service training was scheduled on a "stupid" day and they are not sure they will attend, simply respond with, "You're disappointed that the in-service day interferes with your other plans." These responses diffuse their anger and let them know you are listening to them. You change nothing, you promise nothing; you simply listen and repeat their words back to them. If they push you for action, you reply, "You are really frustrated because of this in-service training day and you really want me to change it. Thanks for letting me know." Again, validate their actions and feelings, but make no commitment; don't even say, "I'll get back to you."

When you validate their concerns, hijackers will feel they have been *heard*. Half of all problems become even larger problems when those who have them feel they have not heard. Eventually, the problem shifts from the original one to the "You don't listen to me" complaint. At this point, the hijacker often forgets what the original issue was. So by using active listening skills, you listen and take their concerns under advisement, but do *not* commit to changing anything, even though in your *own* time, you might change the training date anyway.

If you do decide to change the date, make sure it is *your* choice and *your* decision, and that you are not changing the date because of the hijacker's concerns. Then notify the hijackers *first* and give credit to them for the great idea. They will beam with pride. No, they have not usurped any *real power* from you, only the perceived power you *chose* to provide to them. *You* maintain the power.

Converting Hijackers

Disarming hijackers and converting them to loyal passengers is a nearly impossible task, because they have a "different religion" and are not likely to be swayed by efforts to understand them. Their mission is to seize the aircraft while in flight and force it to a different destination, or use it for their own purposes. From time to time, however, highly skilled negotiators are able to assess that hijackers are not actually attempting to seize control over the organization; rather they are testing out their dissent so strongly they just appear to be hijackers.

Prisoners can turn into hijackers over time, as they become bored and still feel a passion to do something—stirring up trouble can be one of those things. If a newly converted hijacker can be "heard," and a strong, confident, experienced leader can embrace the hijacker and do everything within her power to negotiate with him, and it works, then these achievements must be learned from and celebrated. Unfortunately, all too often, new leaders and deeply entrenched hijackers can't find a common ground. In these cases, other techniques are needed.

> Some of my strongest advocates now were hijackers when I first arrived. Converting hijackers into pilots is my greatest success as a leader.
>
> —**Paul,** Superintendent

If All Else Fails, Protect Yourself

Given that the priority for hijackers is that you and/or your vision and mission lose, it is important to protect yourself. Recognize that hijackers are not on your side or supporting the current path forward and most likely will never be. Understand they are potentially dangerous—to the vision you have for the school, and even to your personal and professional reputation. Watch your back.

Assume they are out to undermine you and your authority—and plan accordingly. If reasonable attempts have failed, don't waste energy trying to woo them, convince them, or gain their allegiance—they are not to be won over. The energy you spend attempting this depletes the reserve you have for more important activities and it fuels the hijackers, since your attempts let them know they have gotten to you.

Be on alert; have your guard up. Once you are certain of their motives, try not to let your guard down with them—trusting them is the greatest mistake you can make. This is important, especially when they approach you with what appears on the surface to be a good idea or when they appear to actually care about you. Don't be fooled.

Try to not let them get "inside" you; that is, refrain from revealing personal information about yourself or your concerns. If you do, this information could be used against you. Their knowledge of your weaknesses becomes useful information at a later date. For this reason, it is imperative that they not *see you emotional*. If you do start to feel emotional in a conversation with them, find a way to leave the room. If necessary, start coughing and excuse yourself. If you are seen as emotional—they will see it as victory and use the power gained to control you.

Consider that anything said in the presence of a hijacker may be next seen in the newspaper, on TV, or the internet. Assume that everything is being recorded, and be prepared to see what you say aired publicly. It just might happen; so it is important to decide what you are willing to be seen on TV or the internet for. It just might be that there are reasons—like standing up against an unethical or unjust student situation—whistleblowers make these decisions every day.

Be above and beyond reproach. This means you live by your ethical standards and demonstrate them at every opportunity. People will know that you live by these standards, and it will never occur to them that you could be anything other than the most upstanding member of the organization. Why is this so important? There are two reasons: (1) There is nothing for the hijacker to find to bring you down, and (2) your reputation will carry you, should the day come that a hijacker ever tell lies about you (they will).

Admit when you are wrong. If you *do* make a mistake, *admit it* and do so to hijackers in person, on their turf. Believe it or not, this does not disempower you. On the contrary, it makes you stronger, because you are modeling vulnerability and authentic behavior.

PILOT'S LOG

When rebuilding the master schedule of courses, the team decided (while looking at the data) that we should increase the number of college prep courses that our students were taking. We eliminated several non-college prep science classes and added a few more biology and earth science classes. This conflicted however, with the belief of the hijacker in the science department. He insisted "our students" (at this underperforming school) were not able to do well in college prep courses. He asked me to keep the status quo, meaning that half our students took college prep courses and the other half took basic science. I used active listening, but eventually the team decided to stick with our decision to move all students forward. That night he went to the school board and announced his position on live TV. He shared that he did not believe we had enough students who were capable of taking college prep courses. He accused me in particular of setting students up for failure. And you know what? I was perfectly fine with him doing this. Because when you decide what you are willing to go on TV for, it centers you philosophically, and doing the right thing for the right reasons feels good.

(The result of my advocacy? The sections were added and student performance increased greatly the following year.)

–**Trish,** Assistant Principal

Frequent Flyers

Pamela was an administrator who hijacked her own high school. While she started out with the support of many, her poor leadership skills and poor decision making quickly led to her loss of favor. Ultimately, when she was in danger of being fired, she had lost the respect of the central office and the site staff, and that's when she became a hijacker. She enlisted the help of prisoners, because they were already unhappy. They assisted her and then sat back and enjoyed the entertainment (protected as prisoners because they were tenured). Pamela spoke with malice and glee regarding an assistant superintendent's very unfortunate public mistake (when she could have demonstrated support and empathy). She was unpredictable, she undermined her staff's efforts at reform, and she sought to take every pilot at the school down with her when she was being fired. She bad-mouthed the superintendent and enlisted the help of the miserable prisoners to help her overturn the superintendent's decision to fire her. Pamela also used her second language as a mechanism with naïve community members, encouraging them to attack site and central office administrators and accuse them of racism and ignorance.

The superintendent and assistant superintendent were savvy and powerful leaders. They utilized their site copilots and passengers as resources. They trusted certain insiders and did not expose their flight plan with the hijacker until the final hour. They remained publicly respectful while privately planning Pamela's exit scenario.

Deborah said all the right things to everyone's face, but behind their backs, she bad-mouthed them. On more than one occasion, she made anonymous and malicious Facebook and other social media posts designed to harm the professional reputations of those who caused her to feel threatened. When confronted about this behavior, Deborah offered to meet with the individuals she harmed and "work this misunderstanding out," and then made excuses for not attending restorative meetings. Further, she blamed some of her colleagues for their role in publicly identifying her as the person who made the posts, portraying herself as a helpless victim unable to convince others that their acts were inappropriate. Indeed, she was the mastermind behind all the "misunderstandings," including some that involved blameless individuals who had little reason to expect a challenge to their competence. She provided her victims with no warning and no prior discussion of their alleged faults; she just made posts with allegations that her colleagues then needed to defend themselves against.

Think Twice Before Trading a Hijacker
Once you get to know your hijackers, it is best to keep them on staff. If they choose to leave, great. If firing is an option, wonderful. But in schools where staff holds tenure, firing may be close to impossible, so administrators often trade difficult employees with each other through involuntary transfers. I *do not* recommend this practice with hijackers, since it is always better to know what's behind door number two than to be surprised by someone else's hijacker. Remember the famous adage, "The devil you know is better that the devil you don't." It takes a great deal of time to learn to manage a hijacker, but once figured out, they are not threatening, so keeping them is best. The known is always better than the unknown.

This Bears Repeating
Always remember that these folks are not your friends; they do not want to be your friends. *Assume they are out to get you and plan accordingly.*

Frequent Flyer

Kelly is a new pilot and just green enough to not realize that the prisoners see her as too young and inexperienced to be a respected pilot. Kelly is *out there*—she challenges the status quo and when faculty pushes back on her new ideas for technology use, she says, "If I can do it, so can you." She mentors other teachers, encourages them and supports teacher collaboration; she wants everyone to be pilots or at least passengers, not recognizing that politically, there can only be so many pilots in the cockpit and that there will always be some prisoners and hijackers. She has not yet learned that she must manage them, not talk down to them; their resistance is not fleeting but is embedded in their core and they are not easily won over at staff meetings with candy, balloons, and singing "We Are Family." Hijackers don't grunt and groan about the singing—they'll make fun of it—and her.

Unfortunately, the growth Kelly needs is an awareness that prisoners and hijackers exist, and despite her best efforts, they will most likely continue to dissent. For her to think that she can win them over in one staff meeting by asking them all to hold hands and sing "Kumbaya" is naïve. While prisoners will be challenging, hijackers must be managed by a strong experienced pilot and/or removed by the central office. Otherwise, eventually Kelly will lose her innocence. One of the hijackers will attack her integrity, and she'll be devastated. At that point, we'll see the type of flyer Kelly can potentially be. She may decide to move to the passenger slot herself or at the request of central office. It's also possible she'll seek strong mentorship for how to manage difficult people, grow a thick skin, screen her future passengers wisely, and become an amazing pilot.

SPECIAL CASE:
HIJACKERS WHO THINK THEY ARE PILOTS

Hijackers may think they are pilots, and worse yet, some may have convinced others that they are pilots instead of the hijackers that they are. This might be one of the most insidious types of hijackers, because you have to mitigate damages that result from the hijacker having a support base of possibly well-meaning passengers who have bought into their plan to take over the plane.

They may go to greater lengths than your average hijacker, because they believe it's their "calling" to fly the plane at any and all costs, regardless of lost time, lack of safety, or other potential damages. They may even believe their purpose is more important than the organization's mission, vision, or product, and try to "sell" their own vision to anyone who will listen—the most vulnerable being prisoners or even passengers who are feeling disenfranchised and who are more likely to "buy" it. If the support base grows large enough, this type of hijacker can become incredibly dangerous to the school, district, or society at large. (Think of how history's most hated dictators rose to power—most were loved or at least well-respected to begin with.)

Hijackers who think they are pilots go to great lengths to maintain their support base—they understand that base is key to their power and control of the plane. They may use social media to drum up support for their causes, inviting only those who share their views into their online circles (i.e. closed groups on Facebook, private Google groups, closed chat rooms). They know how to use the burnout, anger, and/or the desperation of others in the school or district to their advantage. They are master manipulators: deceitful, vindictive and seasoned at playing people against one another.

–**Whitney Triplett,** *a school counseling specialist in Chicago Public Schools*

Consider **Delores,** who at one point was a tremendous pilot and school counseling advocate in her district. Other school counselors respected her for her advocacy and serving as their "voice." However, after several failed attempts to get a policy passed over many years, she became bitter, disillusioned and cynical. She resorted to hijacking any and all planes leaving the airport (i.e. purposely drumming up opposition to new district policies or initiatives, simply to be vindictive), even "taking hostages" in an attempt to accomplish her goals (i.e. refusing to complete paperwork required by the district until her demands were met).

Bill, the math department chair, had been at the school longer than any other faculty member and had seen 11 principals come and go. Everyone knew that Bill was a constant in an ever-changing school community and he was respected among many. He definitely considered himself the one "true" pilot of the school in the midst of changing leadership. But over the years, Bill had grown resentful of the school district's politics and weary of the many changes that seemed to keep coming. He decided to make it his mission to erode the community's hopes in the newest incoming principal—after all, HE was the REAL pilot. He used his loyal support base to undermine the new principal at every turn.

Valerie served on the high school senior activities committee. Although she wasn't the chair of the committee, she believed she was the pilot because of her position as the senior English teacher. She was furious when the chair suggested using a different, cheaper site for prom, due to budget constraints. Rather than voicing her opinion in a constructive manner, she started a closed Facebook group for senior activities, inviting faculty, students, and parents—everyone except the senior activities committee chair. While she opened the group under the guise of increasing communication about senior activities and everyone assumed the committee chair was looped in. Valerie used the group as a platform for drumming up support for the usual prom site instead.

Shelby, a social studies teacher, was the school's elected union representative. Faculty knew he was a hijacker, but they also believed he was the most knowledgeable person on staff about union issues, so they continued to elect him year after year. Shelby honestly felt that he knew what was best for everyone, so he would advise them on what he thought they should do, while withholding information that didn't support his positions and misleading staff about union issues that suited his purpose. Overall, Shelby exploited his position of power to push his own agenda.

III
Managing the Flight

This section will share additional passenger flying styles; offer lessons learned and comments from the field; and if you aspire to be a pilot, methods by which you can do so.

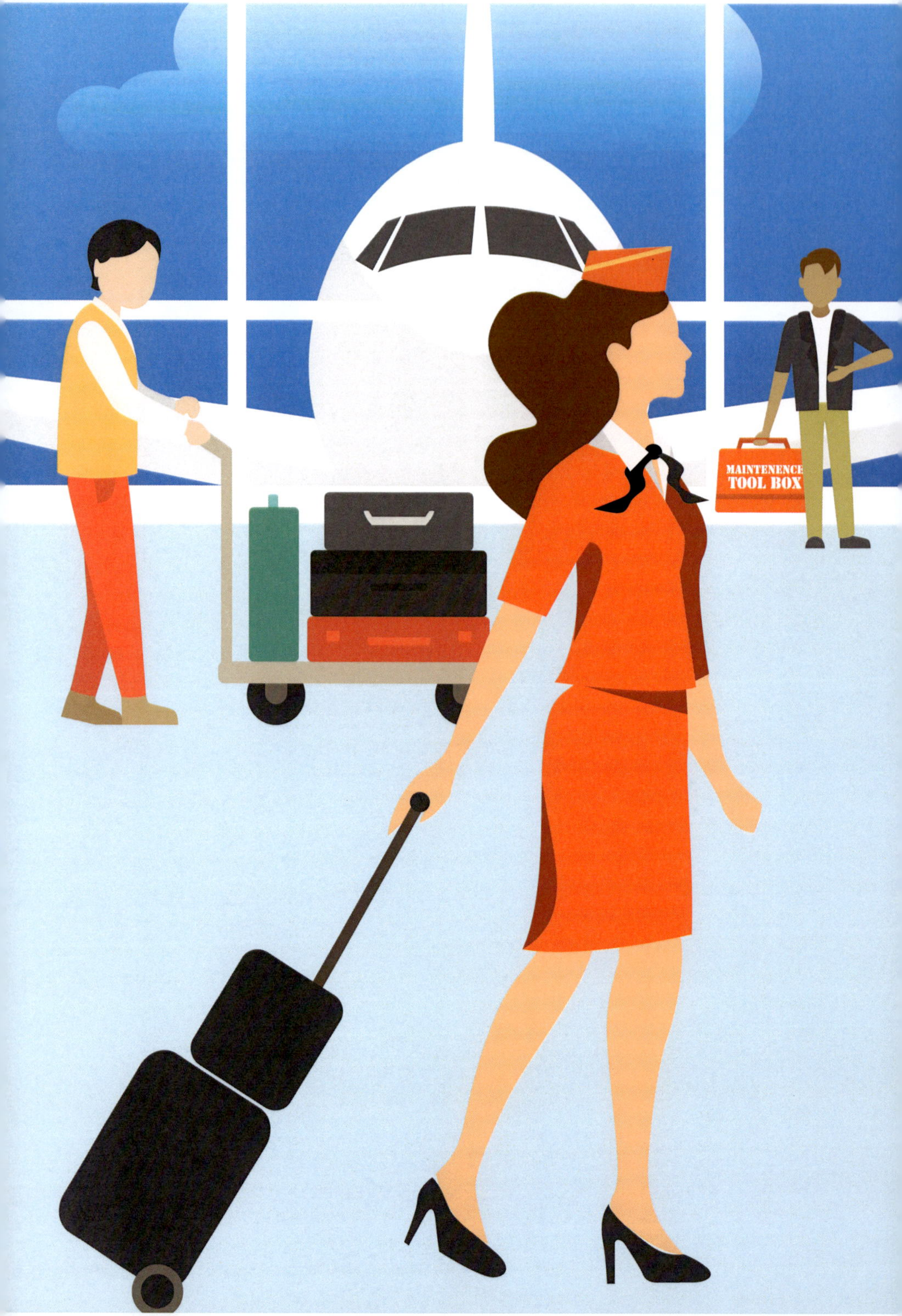
MAINTENENCE
TOOL BOX

7 Other Fellow Passengers

The aeronautical metaphor works for a variety of other roles in schools. The *maintenance crew* are akin to the technicians in *facilities support*. The quicker they come to secure the site after an electrical or gas malfunction, the sooner the plane can take off. *Baggage handlers* are akin to *custodians*—they move the baggage of schools from one room to another, carefully or roughly. *Bus drivers* are akin to the *shuttle drivers* that transport those from parking lots to the airport; their demeanor during that short ride can impact the entire flight.

The chapter covers six other kinds of fellow travelers who deserve special consideration, including copilots; "wannabe" pilots; newborns; flight attendants; passengers in the emergency exit row; and those from the transportation security administration.

COPILOTS

Copilots are a subset of passengers who are a gift to pilots. They assist and support, and occasionally they are given the controls to fly smaller planes in the organization or to take over for the pilot when the pilot takes a break. If pilots are fortunate, they may find they have groomed a terminal copilot: someone who wants a leadership role in the cockpit *with the pilot,* but who does not want to be the first person leading. Just as geese fly in formation, copilots will fall in behind you, but maybe 100% of the direct wind on their noses is a bit much. They prefer instead to draft just a little off you and support you in the process. Many administrators consider them-

> **Frequent Flyer**
>
> **Monica** was as assistant principal (terminal copilot by choice). Although she was offered the pilot's role (to be principal of a school) many times, she preferred to be behind the scenes supporting her principal and working more closely with the staff. She did not enjoy or desire the limelight or front-page rewards or the hassles that went along with being the political "front face" as the person in charge. Rather, Monica preferred, and excelled at, supporting the pilot who did enjoy stepping out in front, feeding her solutions to problems and having her back when needed.

selves "terminal copilots" and that is fine with them. They have just enough leadership opportunity to feel good about the impact they make within the organization, but they have no interest in flying their own plane.

In contrast, watch out for the *non*terminal copilots who still desperately want their own plane. If they don't get it soon, they may start flying in another direction.

"WANNABE" PILOTS

Wannabe pilots hang out by the cockpit looking in at the instrument panel, asking questions and offering advice. They may not be credentialed or trained for this job, but they have seen planes fly on TV or think they are natural-born pilots who might help the pilot in some way. Or perhaps they are former pilots who were demoted and still hold out hope that they will be given another opportunity to be recognized as a pilot.

Every school has at least one wannabe pilot. It is probably a good idea to find an "emergency exit row" job for these wannabe pilots, so they feel important. They need to feel important and if they are ignored long enough, they may become prisoners, or worse, hijackers.

> **Frequent Flyer**
>
> **Renee** is a wannabe pilot blasting out emails about the way it *could be*, and the way it *should be*. She questions: *Why don't we do this or that?* Renee is not a prisoner. She can go to another job, school, or district whenever she wants. The problem, is she just cannot stay in her seat for the ride. She prefers to walk up and down the aisles talking to everyone, and telling them all how to do it a bit better. Renee has no credentials to fly the plane, but she thinks she has a better plan. She's not out to hurt the pilot (and therefore not a hijacker); she just wants to *be* the pilot. Perhaps Renee could be encouraged to attend flight school to see if she'd like to become a pilot but in the meantime, if she's not interested in being a pilot or copilot, Renee should be assigned a job that she is interested in and can do well. This would make her feel important and keep her out of the cockpit.

NEWBORNS

It is a good idea for both pilots and passengers to look out for the newborns (new staff members) in schools. Hijackers are notorious for recruiting among new teachers in schools, districts, or other organizations. By buddying-up to newborns when they are first hired and attempting to give newborns the impression that they are copilots, hijackers gain the allegiance of these newcomers, who can be manipulated later when needed (to get votes, to spy on people, to complain to as victims, etc.). New teachers tend to be naïve and therefore vulnerable as they look for new acquaintances and mentors in their new work environment. Since pilots are busy flying their planes, they are often unaware this is happening. To address this, pilots must alert their trusted copilots to assist and mentor these new individuals, before the newborns are force-fed other ideas by the hijackers.

FLIGHT ATTENDANTS

Who are the flight attendants in schools? Positions may fluctuate and rotate. From time to time, student services personnel may step into these roles and help make the ride safe and comfortable for all on board. Skilled in conflict mediation and diffusion skills, flight attendants do much more than serve drinks. They are highly trained professionals alert to the needs of everyone on the plane. They assist and advise the pilots, support the passengers (in all price categories), and intervene when a crisis occurs and people need help. Good flight attendants provide clear direction and instructions for passengers and create the appropriate "climate" for the plane. Flight attendants are informed and helpful; they ensure passengers' basic needs are met and conflicts are resolved; and they ensure those who are disgruntled (i.e., prisoners) are acknowledged and assisted. In some schools, office staff may also fall into this category.

Flight attendants also know the emergency safety procedures and are always on the lookout for suspicious behavior (potential hijackers). Good fight attendants maintain close collaboration and communication with pilots—addressing needs and providing essential feedback and insight regarding the condition of those on board—to ensure safe takeoffs and landings for every journey.

The truth is, however, airplanes actually *can* fly from New York to Los Angeles without a flight attendant—not as comfortably, but they can get there (which may be why school counselors are sometimes employed in schools and sometimes not, but that's another story).

Therefore, it is vital that those in the flight attendant role feel supported, valued and appreciated. They should also be paid well and held accountable. When they are not, the ride is problematic for all. (Recent headlines about problems with passengers being dragged off flights or mistreated might have been avoided if the support staff were better trained, well compensated, held accountable, and appreciated.)

PASSENGERS IN THE EMERGENCY ROW
Just as on an airplane there are passengers with special responsibilities (such as those sitting by the exit door), so every school, district, or organization has their own "emergency row," where passengers who have spare potential are needed. These seats are perfect for department chairs or those just beginning to lead and wanting practice, willing to do a little more because they want to help, or because there is something in it for them (such as extra money). Those seated in the exit row also get a small perk, such as extra leg room—a great benefit for a little leadership. As mentioned above, it may be helpful to consider placing a wannabe pilot in the emergency row.

TRANSPORTATION SECURITY ADMINISTRATION (TSA) OFFICERS
I fly a great deal and lately, TSA baggage checkers remind me of the school resource officers (SROs) in schools. The responsibility of the SROs is to provide the same safety on campus that the TSA workers provide in the airport. They monitor traffic, check lockers, escort individuals to the office, and break up altercations. At some schools, they even have baggage metal detectors and students are "wanded" on their way to class. If the situation requires a higher level of support, they may call police to the school, much as TSA may call the FBI to the airport. When the security level goes up (orange, red, etc.) a higher level of support and protection is needed.

Pilots recognize and appreciate SROs as an important part of their team to ensure the school moves forward safely and on time.

Like flight attendants, TSA officers must be well trained, monitored and held accountable, as well as appreciated for their hard and sometimes difficult work. Their ability to manage challenging passengers will go a long way toward keeping the airplane out of the news.

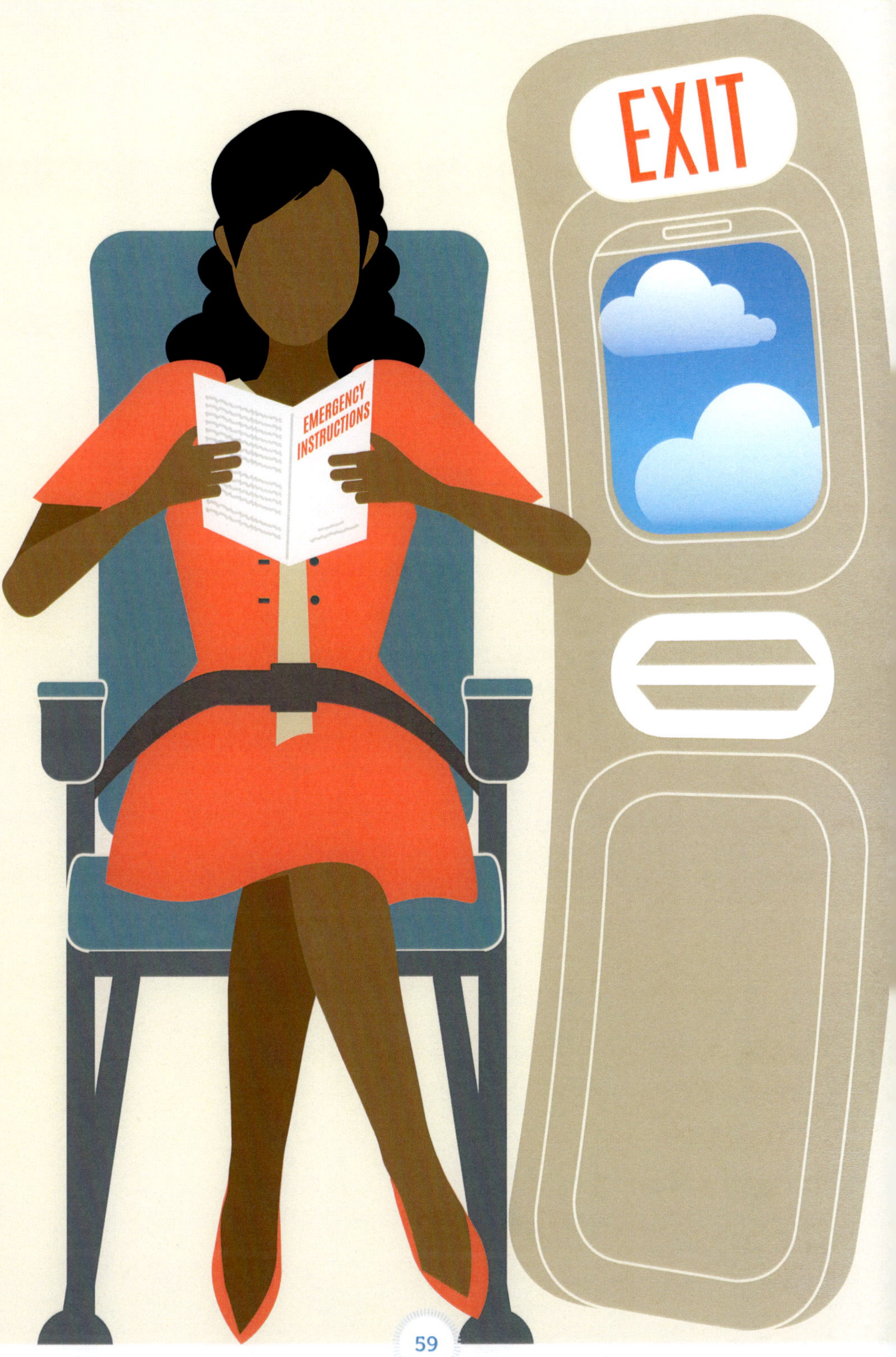
EXIT
EMERGENCY INSTRUCTIONS

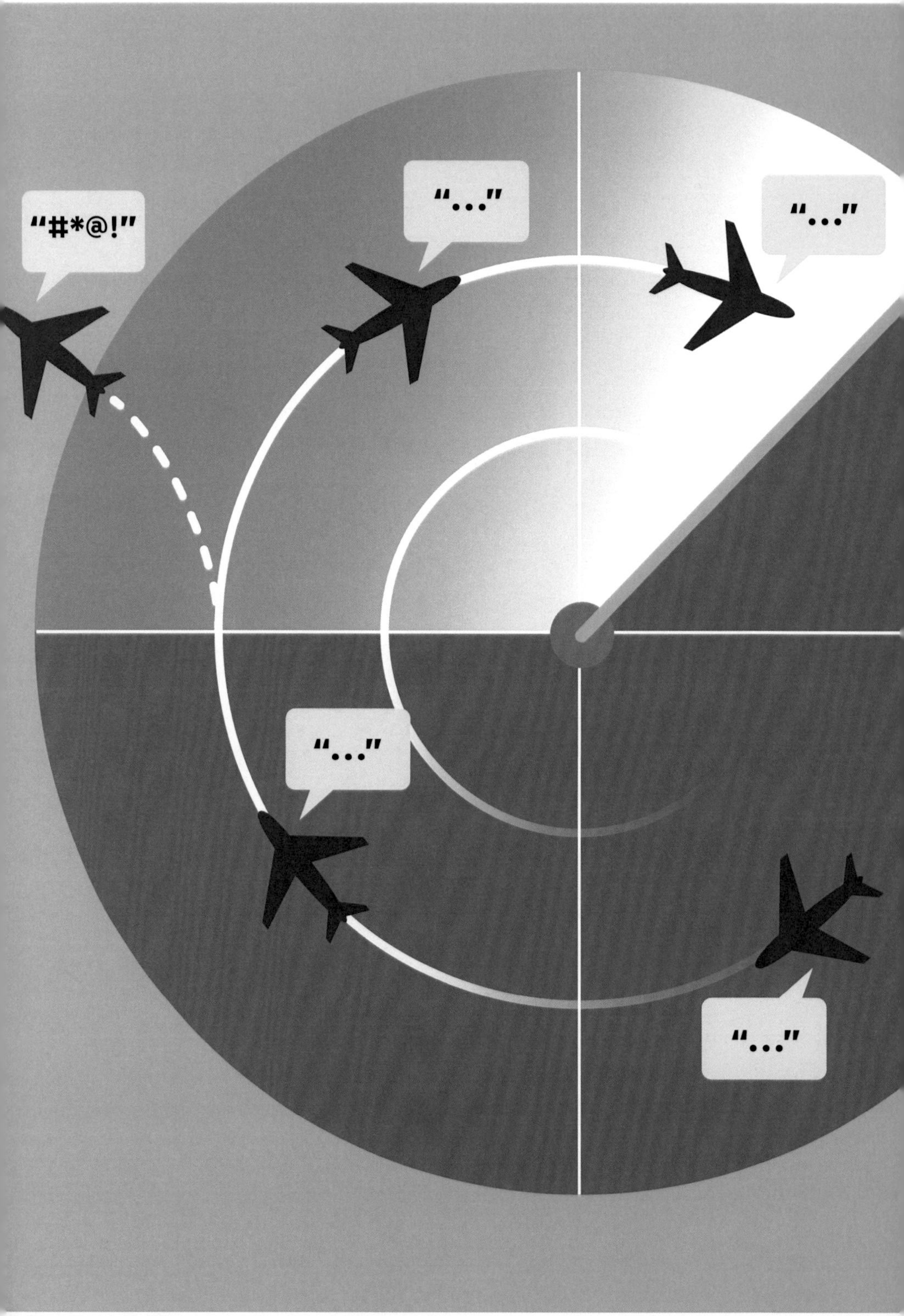

8 Lessons, Questions, and Comments from the Field

Over the past decade I have presented numerous workshops and conference presentations about working with the people on the plane. Some of their most useful questions are presented here, along with my responses.

NO COPILOT FOR ME!

Q: "Help! I am the lead pilot and I have no idea how to take my hands off the controls. I do not know how to fail, as failure for me is never an option. I live on pressure and the thrill of the challenge. I set the highest expectations for myself and those around me. (I ask more, and I get more—I think). I do not trust others to pilot—it's about quality and credibility. I must do it myself. It's all about *me*!"

A: This is a serious concern. Even the best pilots must eat, sleep and use the facilities occasionally. Pilots are notorious for burning out and you are on a flight path to crash! I recommend you select the best copilots you can find, teach them everything you are afraid they don't know, and then begin the task of letting go, slowly at first. When you realize a copilot can fly the plane (come on, how many schools are maintained—some would say "run"—by the secretary, anyway?), you might allow yourself to reflect on the real reasons behind your intense need to control the plane. In the mean time, I would rather not be on your plane!

RELUCTANT PILOTS

Q: "I am naturally a passenger, except in situations where no one steps forward to take on the pilot role in a critical situation. Typically, my role becomes one of an excellent copilot. I want to be a knowledgeable, integral team player and effective supporter of the leader in reaching goals. However, I shy away from the lead role and its intense exposure. If I ever feel particularly passionate about an issue, I have and would welcome being a reluctant pilot, but only for a limited time. In my passenger role, I have enjoyed and learned the importance of self-care and balance in setting realistic goals and balancing my role with those of others. How do I send a message that I do not want to be recruited as a pilot anymore?"

A: This teacher is in a quandary. She wants to be helpful, but she doesn't want to be a pilot. To resolve this, she must be honest with the pilot (principal). A simple conversation is all that is necessary, something like this: "Hello Mr./Ms./Dr. Pilot: I appreciate that you see leadership qualities in me and have enough faith in me to ask that I take on leadership roles within the school. However, I am very comfortable with my current role as a teacher and am not interested in any additional responsibilities, unless a crisis in the school necessitates it. Then, of course, you know I would assist. But lacking an emergency, I am not looking to become a leader within this school in any capacity other than within my classroom. Thank you so much for your faith in me. I promise to continue to support your efforts to move this school forward."

Frequent Flyer

When you have the skill, sometimes you have to fly the plane even when you don't want to. **Rich was a pilot sometimes,** but he much preferred to be a passenger. When his pilot became unable to fly, Rich took over and flew the plane so it didn't crash.

Rich is this type of guy—not a natural-born leader; he would never seek to fly the plane on his own. But when confronted with the option of crashing or landing, Rich took over the controls. Rich was so uncomfortable leading as a pilot, that he refused to come to meetings without his copilots.

POTENTIAL HIJACKERS

Q: "I think I might be a potential hijacker. Sometimes I feel so headstrong about my opinions, I don't listen to others. I feel a burning need to hijack the new person who is now in charge. Do you have any suggestions for me?"

A: Yes, you might want to seek mentorship from pilots that you respect and confide in them. Seek guidance from experienced pilots who have seen it all and can offer assistance. If staying is not possible, then consider flying your own plane. This often happens with assistant principals. They start out as very supportive, helpful, dedicated allies of the pilot (and the district office). Eventually, many become impatient if they are not promoted when they believe they are ready, and their need to control their own plane takes on a passion that interferes with their allegiance to the current pilot. They then fall into the "potential hijacker" category. At that time, it is good for them to find their own plane to fly—out of another airport if necessary.

PILOT "SECRETARIES"

Q: "Help! My secretary is a passenger—worse yet, I think she might be a prisoner. (Thank goodness she's not a hijacker.) The frustrating thing is, I need her to be a copilot, so she can run things when I am not around. My friend has a pilot secretary."

A: This is another real quandary. Pilots fortunate enough to have a copilot secretary are blessed, but typically this is not the case. If secretaries wanted to be pilots, they would have chosen that profession. While there are some secretaries who are pilots to others (lead secretary), many chose the role of secretary because they like supporting others in their leadership role but do not want be the one in charge. To ask them to be pilots when this was not their intent is an unfair expectation. This is where many pilots fail—they have unreasonable expectations of their secretaries, expecting them to take over control of the plane without any of the formal training!

Secretaries who are truly are serving in the pilot's role are often doing so because their boss is a passenger by nature, or perhaps the boss is asleep at the wheel. Another possibility is that the secretary is a born pilot who never got her credentials and now leads vicariously. Neither is a good scenario. Having two "first" pilots does not work and a principal who puts this level of trust in a non-certified staff member will cause concern among the passengers.

PARACHUTING

Q: "I have a hard time staying out of my pilot's way and letting him do his job. I know he thinks I am a hijacker. I realize that it is his job and his responsibility (even when the plane is on autopilot) and I am uncomfortable with my uneasiness when I disagree with the pilot. I do not want my own plane and do not want to crash his. What can I do?"

A: First, talk with your pilot and share your ambition. Ask for help in supporting your career goals. Perhaps you could be allowed to be a "test pilot" in certain areas; that is, you could try out your different ideas for a single grade or department or project in the school.

Also, it is important to remember that qualified pilots need support, but they also benefit from honest feedback. People in positions of authority can and must be called into question when events occur that are serious or dangerous. Knowing how and when to address these issues is an important talent.

However, if you are unable to provide constructive and appropriate feedback; are dead-set on disagreeing with the pilot in charge (over issues that are not serious); and you find yourself complaining in a nonproductive (potentially damaging) manner; you have two choices: you can either reform your behavior, sit quietly, assist others in having a safe and comfortable flight, wait until the flight is over and get off (i.e., seek a transfer at the end of the school year); or you can parachute (quit). Either way, you must stay out of the pilot's way, or everyone on the plane will suffer.

CHANGING ROLES

Q: "I have found that I play different roles with different people. For instance, in most projects I am a pilot, completing any task my principal or superintendent asks of me. However, when I am with my guidance director, I find myself turning into a hijacker. I feel she doesn't appreciate me and isn't aware of my talents and when she asks me to do things, well…you know what hijackers do."

A: You have pointed out a very common problem for pilots. Pilots respond to appreciation, and your guidance director is not seeing your gifts and how you are contributing. On the other hand, she is the designated pilot for guidance activities—*she* is the guidance director. Therefore, when you are working with her, you are by definition a copilot at best. If you are on a small plane, it may even be a single-seater up front, with no room for you.

Reread what pilots need, try to meet her needs and see if these actions help the two of you get along better. Then, ascertain whether she is looking for a copilot. If she is, take your orders and support her. If she is not, then, in this situation, you are a passenger. You can stay on the plane and be a passenger, become a prisoner or hijacker, or get off that plane and onto another one. After all, for now, this is *her* flight. Remember, however, that if you are patient, the pilot may eventually leave on her own, or be transferred. If you are determined to stay (you like the airline) then patience must prevail.

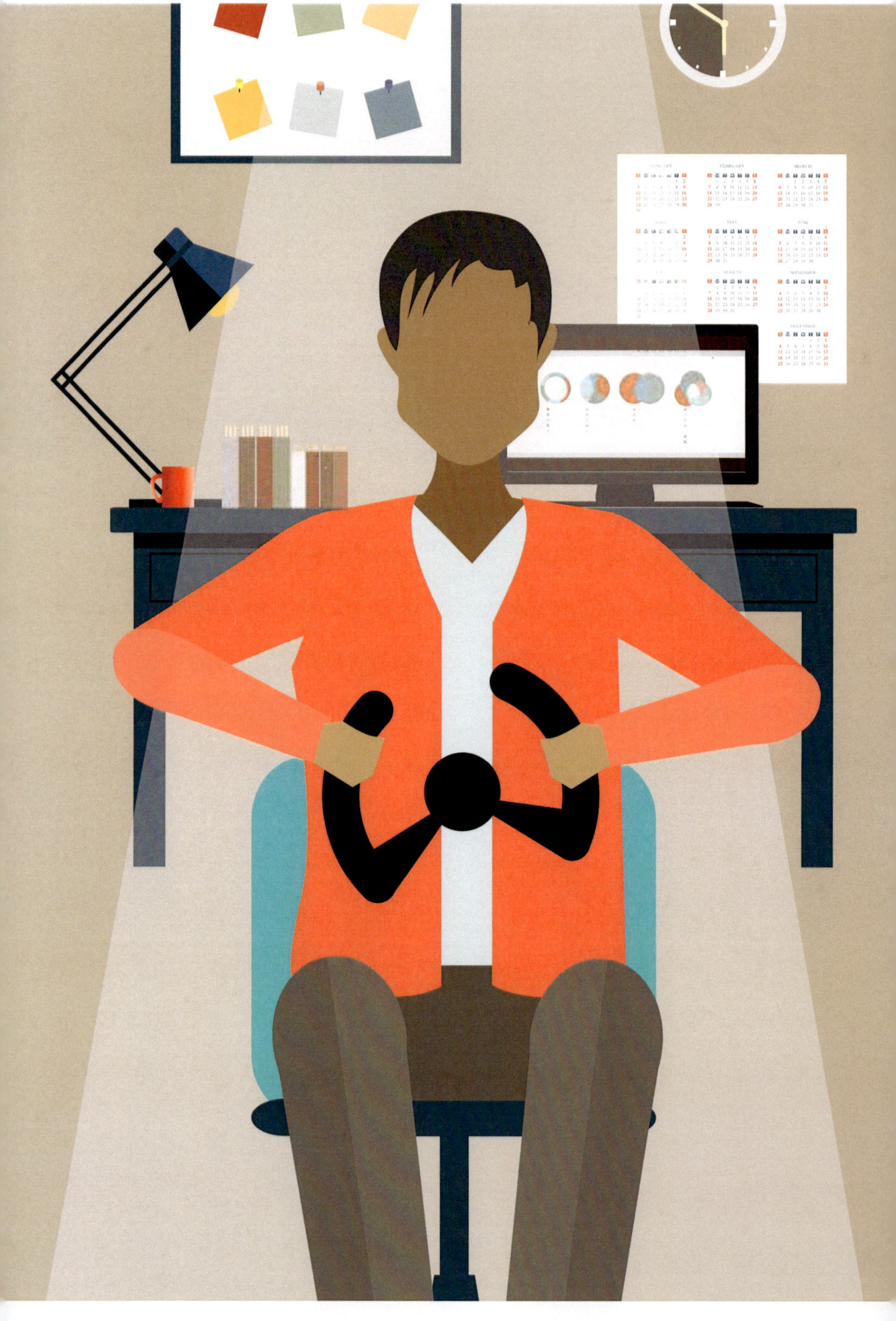

9 So You Want to Be a Pilot?

EXCELLENCE IN LEADERSHIP

Truly gifted leaders can predict the situation in which each of the archetypes will emerge and will plan to work with each of them optimally. They will know how to reinforce those who need it. They see (and feel) this instinctively, and will devise a plan of action to determine which of the techniques listed in Section II they will use to ensure effective forward movement within the organization. They may also do this to fend off a potential takeover or to empower passengers.

While this ability is in part a skill that pilots can learn, it is difficult to teach. While knowing what to do can be taught, the ability to predict when specific action is necessary may be more of a gift. However, the more experience you have, the better you become at predicting the needs within your organization. Over time, you can maximize your potential to be a "gifted" leader by melding your instincts with your learning experiences. You will tend to improve when you pay attention to both your gut and your life lessons. After a while, this process may become almost automatic for you.

> My principal is a pilot.
> And everyday when I leave he says:
> "Thanks for a good day."
> I truly believe this helps improve school climate.
>
> —**Jill,** *School Teacher*

GROOMING NEW PILOTS

As you develop your experience as a pilot, one of the greatest gifts you can give is to mentor new pilots. An experienced and respected pilot best fulfills the responsibility of supporting an up-and-coming pilot. If you happen to be a gifted pilot, consider giving back. Excellence in leadership also means selecting the correct copilots, who may be assistants of any kind—secretaries, vice principals, supportive classroom teachers. Some pilots are very good at grooming wonderful copilots. If you have carefully selected copilots with different talents and abilities, you can truly trust that you are in good hands if it is ever necessary to let go of the wheel for a short time. When everyone is flying in formation, organizations are able to move forward very quickly.

But as with all true pilots, eventually the copilots you are mentoring will want to have their own airplane, so transfers are inevitable. While it may be frustrating to have your copilots leave as soon as they are trained, it is all part of the growth process. If you are considering becoming a pilot, check out the credentials of your mentor pilot carefully. Look into the percentage of on-time arrivals, and seek insight from others who have been passengers or worked closely with the pilot (flight attendants). You deserve the best mentor and the world needs more excellent pilots.

PUSHING PASSENGERS TOO HARD

Overzealous pilots may make the mistake of deciding that everyone is as excited to fly as much as they are. They may assign staff to take on mini-leadership roles on projects without checking to see if they are interested in a leadership opportunity. It's important to remember that if passengers wanted to be pilots, they probably would be. When moved out of their comfort zone, people often respond in ways pilots don't expect.

Try not to push passengers too hard; or they might become prisoners, or worse, hijackers. We all have read about parents who push (force or press upon) children too hard, and what happens? Sometimes the children rebel. Take time to assess the interest level of passengers, and then select wisely. Know when to ask for help. As mentioned before, if passengers are loyal to you, they will step up and assist when needed in a crisis situation. However, if passengers discover that you believe every problem is a crisis that they must assist with immediately, they will lose faith in you. Therefore, be careful not to hit the emergency button too many times. Select the right times to ask passengers for help.

IF YOU ARE ON THE WRONG PLANE, *GET OFF*

When you get on the plane, you know the flight attendant routine: "This is the 6:30 flight to _____. If you are not going to _____, then you need to deplane." We all have a ticket. It tells us where we are going.

To know where you're going, it is important to create a mission statement for your organization. Everyone does better if you are all on the same page. At the first staff meeting of the year, principals lead with the goals and objectives for the year clearly outlined. This is a good time to see if the plane is headed in the direction you want to go.

If you are on the wrong plane and unable to support the destination it is headed in, get off. If it's too late to get off this flight, then shift flights or airlines at the next opportunity. Staying on board too long with a pilot you don't want to travel with, heading to a destination you don't want to go to, will surely transform you into a prisoner, which could have unfortunate outcomes, especially once it's time to ask for a recommendation to transfer. Rather than disrupt all on board, stay patient, make a plan and get support to move to a different plane—one that's going where you want to go.

GET COMMITMENT FROM THE SQUADRON BEFORE TAKING OFF

Imagine that each department in the school (math, English, etc.) has its own small plane and that all departments are able to fly in formation as a unit (school). Now imagine that one department creates a new map and heads off in a different direction. The result would be that the school gets off course as a whole.

For example, imagine that all the core departments (math, social studies, science, English) in a school publicly support changing the registration packet to support more rigorous coursework (more college prep) for 9th-grade students, and that these same core departments want to modify the prerequisite requirements for these college-prep courses, to allow for greater equity and access for all students to a more thorough education. Imagine also that the staff of one department in this school decides they do not endorse this new policy. This one department's philosophy would conflict with the messages sent by the other departments, which encourage students to take rigorous courses. The philosophical dissent would stall and perhaps hijack the forward movement of the entire unit (school).

If all the parts of a unit are not using the same map and flying together (preferably in formation), the unit runs the risk of going in more than one direction, thus stalling forward progress. Can you picture the person in the band or on the football team who suddenly puts aside the routine or playbook and decides to go his or her own direction, while everyone else is following the formation? Regardless of your opinion on this particular issue (students taking rigorous courses), the lack of unity in the school staff is a greater concern. It impacts the ability to move forward.

Therefore, a good leader goes over the flight plan with the squadron and confirms their commitment to the destination before taking off. This is not to say that innovation won't sometimes require small adjustments during flight. Schools typically can't land for a year and then reconsider their course before taking off again. Sometimes it's necessary to adjust the flight plan while the plane is flying. In this case, however, it is still necessary that those in leadership roles support the adjustment. This way, everyone is attending to warning signs that things aren't going well and the team works together to ensure a safe landing for all.

MANAGING THE MISSION

Once you are confident you are on the right plane, that you have chosen co-pilots and flight attendants well, and that everyone is on board, you can take off. Make sure those flying in formation with you are ready to take off too.

Check in with them at the beginning of the flight and then once more toward the end—just to let them know you are there. If there is turbulence, let them know right away that you are there, in charge, and everything is okay. Or, share that the turbulence is temporary and expected, and that you are confident it will end soon. Not knowing outcomes scares passengers.

Spend some time with hijackers (if you know where they hang out). Remember, keep your friends close and your enemies closer.

Be available at the end of the flight, so others can thank you for a job well done. (They like thanking you.)

Stay calm, cool and collected, even when the plane is actually crashing—and if that is the case, lead all the passengers, prisoners and hijackers in prayer; don't panic or abandon them. During this time, they need you to be strong. And calm is strength!

10 The Right Formula

> **RESEARCH SO FAR**
>
> Can we pre-flight check a school or organizational system to determine if there is any correlation between the ratio of prisoners and hijackers to pilots/passengers and the performance of a school? What is the ratio in high-performing schools? You might at first think having a lot of pilots is a good thing. But consider that the cockpit is only so big—only so many can fit into it—so the answer is probably not that you have a lot of pilots, but rather that you have fewer hijackers and prisoners.

WHAT IS THE "RIGHT" FORMULA?

At a national conference, school counselors and administrators answered the following questions: (1) Rate your school from 1-to-10 on a scale, with 1 being the lowest performing and 10 being the highest performing, and (2) indicate your best guess at the number (and/or percentage) of pilots, passengers, prisoners and hijackers at your school site. The preliminary and admittedly nonscientific results suggest a small but significant and positive correlation between reported school achievement and the percentage of pilots (.38) and passengers (.33). This indicates that *as school achievement increases, so too do the numbers of pilots and passengers*. Slightly larger correlations were observed between the reported number of prisoners (-.53) and hijackers (-.42) and school achievement. These negative correlations indicate that *as the numbers of prisoners and hijackers increase, school achievement decreases*. All correlations are significant at the $p < .01$ level.

This was a small and preliminary study ($N = 76$). Additional reliable and valid research is planned to determine whether additional study is needed, but it is safe to assume that the fewer hijackers and prisoners you have, the better. It probably doesn't matter how many passengers you have; rather it's the ratio of passengers to pilots, prisoners and hijackers that matters most.

TOO MANY PILOTS?

This often happens. In such cases, it is great to create more copilots. Or, better yet, create more airplanes and put the copilots in charge of different projects (sort of their own single-engine airplane, e.g., department chair). Don't forget that they need praise, praise, praise.

NOT ENOUGH PILOTS?

Not having enough pilots or copilots is a problem, because then pilots have to do it all themselves, or give tasks to those who don't follow through. There is nothing worse than assigning tasks to those (passengers) who then take their time to complete them. It can be frustrating, because the passengers are in no rush (or at least not in the same rush as the pilot is). It's important to remember that for passengers, their ego is *not* dependent on this task completion or on making the pilot look good. Refer to Chapter 4 for strategies on how to make the most of passengers.

You can never have too few prisoners or hijackers, but if your ratio runs a little high, here are some things to consider.

TOO MANY PRISONERS?

Review Chapter 5 for strategies on working with prisoners. While working toward options for getting them on to a different plane, treat them with compassion and support to minimize their pain and help them perform as well as they can.

TOO MANY HIJACKERS?

As discussed in Chapter 6, it doesn't work to transfer hijackers. Your best option is to get to know them well, praise them when possible and keep them close.

THE RIGHT FORMULA

Who's On This Flight With You?

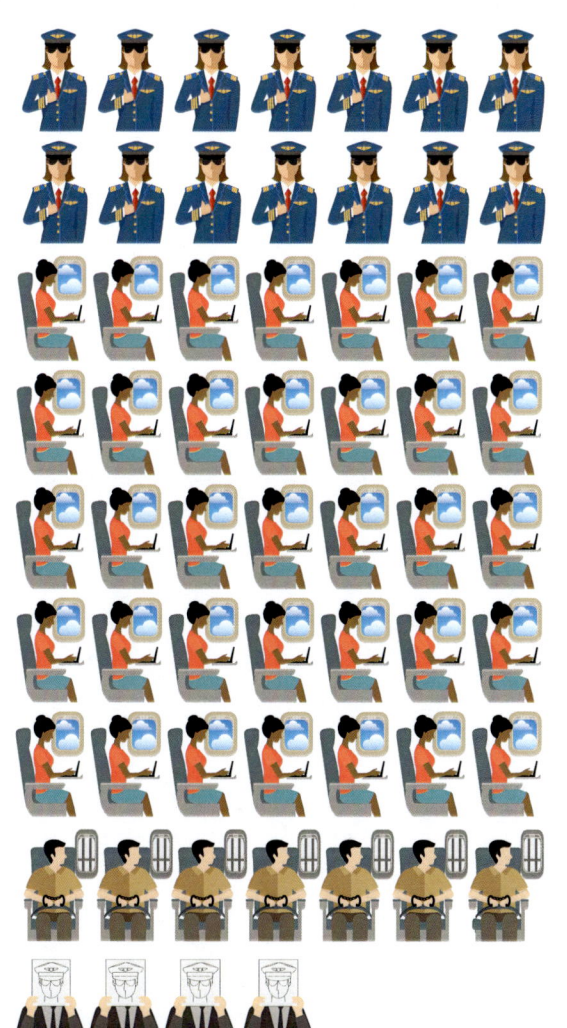

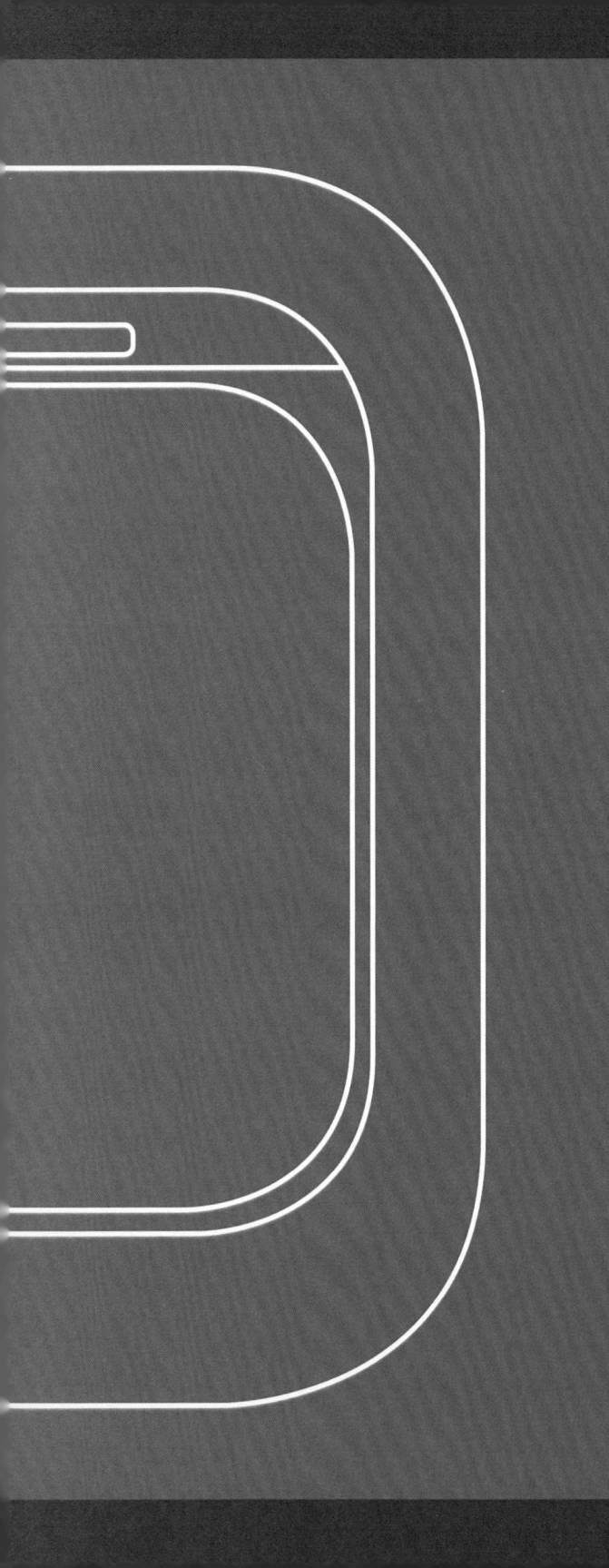

Appendices

Here you will find 8 different activities to refine your understanding of the archetypes, as well as charts and word clouds that explore the common "wants" and "needs" of each archetype.

APPENDIX I

Activity Worksheets

ACTIVITY #1

WHO UPSETS YOU THE MOST?

List the names (or pseudonyms) of individuals in your school, organization, or business who you *have difficulty getting along with* and the *actions they perform* (or don't perform) that *you find most upsetting or disturbing*.

Name: _____ Action: _____

_____

Name: _____ Action: _____

_____

Name: _____ Action: _____

_____

Name: _____ Action: _____

_____

Name: _____ Action: _____

_____

ACTIVITY #2

WHO DO YOU KNOW WHO IS ... ?

List the names of people you believe are in each archetype.

Pilots:

_____
_____
_____
_____

Passengers:

_____
_____
_____
_____

Prisoners:

_____
_____
_____
_____

Hijackers:

_____
_____
_____
_____

ACTIVITY #3

WHAT HAS WORKED?

Strategies I have tried that *have worked* with:

Pilots:

_____
_____
_____
_____

Passengers:

_____
_____
_____
_____

Prisoners:

_____
_____
_____
_____

Hijackers:

_____
_____
_____
_____

ACTIVITY #4

WHAT HAS NOT WORKED?

Strategies I have tried that *have NOT worked* with:

Pilots:

_____
_____
_____
_____

Passengers:

_____
_____
_____
_____

Prisoners:

_____
_____
_____
_____

Hijackers:

_____
_____
_____
_____

ACTIVITY #5

THIS WEEK I'LL TRY...

Strategies I will try this week with:

Pilot: (list name) _____

_____

_____

_____

_____

Passenger: (list name) _____

_____

_____

_____

_____

Prisoner: (list name) _____

_____

_____

_____

_____

Hijacker: (list name) _____

_____

_____

_____

_____

ACTIVITY #6

WHERE IS YOUR PLANE HEADED?

1. Are you on course?

2. If not, where is your plane headed that you do not want to see it go to?

3. Is there potential that it might crash? Why?

4. Are you being hijacked? By whom?

5. What is the hijacker doing?

6. What can you do to redirect it... *now*?

7. How will you know you are back on course?

ACTIVITY #7

DIFFERENT SITUATIONS

Do you respond differently in different scenarios? For each of the situations shown below, circle the role you play.

1. At work?   Pilot   Passenger   Prisoner   Hijacker

2. At home?   Pilot   Passenger   Prisoner   Hijacker

3. When visiting relatives?   Pilot   Passenger   Prisoner   Hijacker

4. In social situations?   Pilot   Passenger   Prisoner   Hijacker

5. In the community?   Pilot   Passenger   Prisoner   Hijacker
(Watching children's sports, in church groups, Kiwanis, volunteer work, etc.)

6. In other situations?   Pilot   Passenger   Prisoner   Hijacker
(List other situations below: _____.)

ACTIVITY #8

MY PILOT IMPROVEMENT WORKSHEET

1. My current mentees:

2. My list of potential copilots:

3. My methods for appreciating others:

4. My list of self-care activities:

APPENDIX II

What do Flyers FEEL?
What do Flyers WANT?

P³H has been presented in keynotes and conference workshops or trainings to thousands of educators, administrators and school counselors. Many presentations have been followed by activity sessions where participants are asked to think of a time when they embodied an archetype in P³H. They are then asked to form a group with others who identify with the same archetype as they do and to respond to the following questions: *What do you feel? What do you want?* The words in the charts in this section represent the most common responses collected during these activities by participants.

As leaders, it is helpful to understand where our followers are coming from, so when we hear these words, we can be supportive by identifying empathetically with the feelings and desires of different faculty members who embody the characteristics these words represent. Leaders in educational organizations might find it helpful to discuss these groups of words as a starting activity with their faculty or organization, before discussing the examples in Section II.

Getting together to talk about feelings and wants prior to starting other activities, might be a beneficial way to have enlightening, candid conversations. Rather than judging or blaming, this discussion would be more about understanding perspectives and gaining ideas and strategies to support and empower all members of an organization who are sharing a plane, in an attempt to make the flight as comfortable as possible until the destination is reached.

inspiration
growth relationships
included respect
balanced
comfortable
peace
valued appreciated voice
relief
leadership
flexibility direction structure
communication
support balance
consistency
independence

PILOTS REPORT FEELING:

Empowered	Optimistic	Ownership	Change	Visionary
Responsible	Desire	Overwhelmed	Frustrated	Anxious
Driven	Unappreciated	Productive	Gratified	Alone
Exhausted	Confident	Purposeful	Enthusiastic	Passionate
Excited	Perfectionist	Competent	Organized	Accomplished
Pressure	Control	Balance	Everybody is watching	

When displayed in a "word cloud," which shows the size of each word based on the frequency with which it is used, pilots' most common **feelings** are represented as follows:

PILOTS REPORT WANTING:

To be trusted	Common vision	Outcomes	Validation	To be competent
Positivity	Appreciation	Control	Support	Help
Shared passion	Respect	Team	Change	Participation
Commitment	Accountability	Efficiency	Others to do things the right way	
Things to be done right the first time		Everyone to be the best she or he can be		
To be seen as the heart of the school		To have the best job		To enjoy work
Other people to step up to the plate		Others to offer help without me having to ask		
Shared responsibility		Others to stop saying, "It's not my job"		

When displayed in a word cloud, pilots' most common **wants** are represented as follows:

support
appreciation help
recognition
passion
commitment respect
control validation
positivity
trust team
competency
efficiency
change common vision
participation
outcomes
accountability

PASSENGERS REPORT FEELING:

Overwhelmed	Frustrated	Targeted	Stressed	Content
Comfortable	Relaxed	Responsible	Direction	Balanced
Agreeable	Accommodating	Predictable	Supportive	Safe
Empathetic	Willing	Indifferent	Secure	Satisfied
Competent	Protective	Shy	Scared	Ignorant
Committed	Needed	Freedom	Tired	Overwhelmed
Flexible	Unsure	Used	Calm	Apathetic
Along for the ride	No longer want to be pilot			

When displayed in a word cloud, passengers' most common **feelings** are represented as follows:

PASSENGERS REPORT WANTING:

To have voice	Support	Relief	Structure	Respect
Consistency	Relationships	Balance	To be included	Inspiration
Direction	Independence	Growth	To be left alone	Flexibility
To be valued	To be appreciated	Stronger leadership	No interruptions	Things to go smoothly
To stop being asked to do other people's jobs				

When displayed in a word cloud, passengers' most common **wants** are represented as follows:

inspiration
growth relationships
included respect
peace
valued appreciated voice
relief **leadership**
flexibility direction structure
communication
balance
support
consistency
independence

PRISONERS REPORT FEELING:

Apathetic	Frustrated	Angry	Misunderstood	Disconnected
Defeated	Trapped	Unappreciated	Impatient	Depressed
Overwhelmed	Inadequate	Stuck	Useless	Lost
Helpless	Resentful	Disappointed	Discouraged	Tired
Lifeless	Invisible	Hostile	Separated	Overlooked
Helpless	Powerless	Unmotivated	Frustrated	Burnt out
Manipulated	Unsupported	Resentful	Despair	Separated
Squashed	Ignored	Spiteful	Dread	Stifled
Silent	Ineffective	Stretched	Anxious	Sad
Lack of control	Misconception of power			

When displayed in a word cloud, prisoners' most common **feelings** are represented as follows:

PRISONERS REPORT WANTING:

To be appreciated	To be included	To have a voice	To leave on time	To have an impact
To be happy	To get out	To seek refuge	To be noticed	To be recognized
To get attention	To gain positioning	Stronger leadership	To have affirmation	To be empowered
To be valued	Respect	Support	Combat pay	Direction
To see change	Independence	To be left alone	To retire	Smart kids
Someone else to fix it	A different experience	To be understood	To have a lunch hour	To experience success
Others to see value in their abilities	To not be told what to do	To not be micromanaged	Others to stop coming up with new ideas	

When displayed in a word cloud, prisoners' most common **wants** are represented as follows:

leadership understanding **recognition** empowerment valued affirmation appreciated success respect **voice** noticed impact understood change support included refuge out attention happiness independence positioning direction

HIJACKERS REPORT FEELING:

Fear	Creative	Vindictive	Tired	Unhappy
Convincing	Insecure	Confident	Angry	Resentful
Justified	Unappreciated	Threatened	Defensive	Frustrated
Isolated	Oppositional	Right	Protective	Attacked
Misunderstood	Envious	Disrespected	Responsible	Cynical
Anxious	Subversive	Tenacious	Alone	Overlooked
Idealistic	Knowledgeable	Superior	Control	Like leaders
Helpless	Different	We are the voice of those who don't speak up			
We would make better pilots		Inability to make change			
My school, my rules		Pilot on my own agenda		We are always right
Don't need or want change		I have all the answers			
We are the voice of prisoners		We are pissed-off pilots			
We have the skills to be pilots		Different views are squashed			
My way or the highway		We could be great leaders			
We need other hijackers because we cannot operate on our own				

When displayed in a word cloud, hijackers' most common **feelings** are represented as:

HIJACKERS REPORT WANTING:

Control	To have voice	Responsibility	Respect	Justice
Recognition	Acknowledgement	Change	Validation	Consistency
Revenge	Security	To be the pilot	To stir the pot	Destruction
Our way or no way				

When displayed in a word cloud, hijackers' most common **wants** are represented as follows:

> voice
> respect
> responsibility security
> consistency control revenge
> recognition
> validation change
> acknowledgement
> justice

Note that in the case of the hijacker, while there are very few "wants" reported, they are *very* clear about *what* they want.

ACKNOWLEDGMENTS

I first conceptualized the Pilots, Passengers, Prisoners and Hijackers (P3H) paradigm nearly two decades ago while–ironically–on an airplane after leading a training session. Since drafting my initial outline of the four standard archetypes, I've shared, revised and continued to expand upon this concept dozens of times for the basis of various keynote speeches and training courses I've given around the country.

Over the years, I've been fortunate to receive supportive and positive input from numerous colleagues and those I've presented P3H to in various keynote or training settings. Many encouraged me to share these concepts in a book.

I completed my text and shared it with several publishers who, although they loved the book and its concept, held concerns for publishing a book with the term "hijacker" on the front cover. I was encouraged to change the term to "saboteur" or "resister" and the like. While I considered this, as Sept. 11, 2001 had forced the idea to a back burner for sensitivity reasons, I couldn't get the other titles to stick. As it turns out, according to those I continues to share the text with, the term "hijacker" was indeed, the most aligned with the metaphor. In the years since, as both a school counselor educator, national trainer and consultant, I continued to utilize the metaphor but resisted publishing until recently, when I was strongly encouraged to self-publish the text. This year, I decided to make that a priority.

I'd first like to thank my brother, Paul Meyers, my mentor and fellow educator, for reading my drafts (many, many times) and giving me his candid, objective and invaluable feedback over the years. I am grateful to those who provided extensive comments, contributions and support including Mariko Cavey, Whitney Triplett, Stuart Chen-Hayes, the San Diego State University graduating class of 2013, several people who provided feedback so long ago that I have since lost their names and contacts (so sorry), and many, many more friends and colleagues (too many to mention) who pushed me over and over to publish–thank you for your persistent encouragement.

To my amazing three sons Brian, Michael and Greg Hatch, for inspiring and supporting me always, I love you! To my Hatching Results "team": Danielle Duarte, Lisa De Gregorio, Trisha McHugh, Whitney Triplett and Vanessa Gomez, THANK YOU for your feedback throughout the process and your undying support for the work we do to support school counselors and the students they serve. To every school counselor or administrator colleague that I've ever worked with, school counselors whom I've educated, and others I have trained, THANK YOU for your feedback, encouragement and letters detailing how this "work" has already helped you to improve your practice in schools.

Special thanks to Cate Huisman for your editorial support and to Morgan M. Hurley, for your editorial guidance and insightful feedback on the layout of the final version. Finally, I'd like to acknowledge with great gratitude Steve Glorioso of Auburn Associates, Inc., in Baltimore, Maryland, whose design expertise brought my concepts and archetypes to life on the printed page.

RESOURCES

Trish Hatch, PhD., is the best-selling author of several books, all available for purchase.

- *Hatching Results for Elementary School Counseling: Implementing Core Curriculum and Other Tier 1 Activities* (Hatch, Duarte & De Gregorio, 2018) — for more information or to purchase, visit bit.ly/2HddiTp
- *The Use of Data in School Counseling* (Hatch, 2014) — visit bit.ly/2J1P98d
- *Evidence-Based School Counseling: Making a Difference with Data-Driven Practices* (Dimmitt, Carey & Hatch, 2007) — visit bit.ly/2sp0EdT
- *ASCA National Model: A Framework for School Counseling Programs* (ASCA 2003, 2005) — visit bit.ly/2J4pzPR

Dr. Hatch's educational consulting business, Hatching Results, LLC, offers short and long-term customized training plans for school administrators, school counselors, and school districts. More information can be found at hatchingresults.com.

Hatching Results also offers facilitated online courses for professional development credit. For more information, visit hatchingresults.com.